The
West Midl
Village Book

THE VILLAGES OF BRITAIN SERIES

Other counties in this series include

Avon*
Bedfordshire*
Berkshire*
Buckinghamshire*
Cambridgeshire
Dorset
Essex*
Gloucestershire*
Hampshire
Herefordshire*
Hertfordshire*
Kent
Leicestershire
  & Rutland*
Middlesex*

Northamptonshire*
Nottinghamshire*
Oxfordshire
Powys Montgomery*
Shropshire*
Somerset*
Staffordshire*
Suffolk
Surrey
East Sussex
West Sussex
Warwickshire*
Wiltshire
Worcestershire*

*Published in conjunction with County Federations
of Women's Institutes

The West Midlands Village Book

Compiled by the West Midlands
Federation of Women's Institutes from notes
and illustrations sent by Institutes in the County

Published jointly by
Countryside Books, Newbury
and the WMFWI, Stechford

First published 1989
© West Midlands Federation of Women's Institutes 1989

Countryside Books
3 Catherine Road
Newbury, Berkshire

ISBN 1 85306 054 2

Cover photograph of Knowle, taken by Mrs Innes Brett

Produced through MRM Associates Ltd., Reading
Typeset by Acorn Bookwork, Salisbury
Printed in England by J. W. Arrowsmith Ltd., Bristol

Foreword

A warm welcome to the County of the West Midlands. To many people, the West Midlands is associated with heavy industry, dirt and grime; but after reading this book I hope it will be appreciated just how much beauty and history abounds here. Truly a County of contrasts. From the very large and bustling City of Birmingham to its tiny little hamlets like Temple Balsall, the home of the Knights Templars, there is so much of interest and variety to see and explore.

WI members have spent a great deal of time in research for this book and gained, I know, enormous pleasure in so doing.

I trust it will whet your appetite. Do come and see for yourselves.

Betty Morgan
County Chairman

County of
WEST MIDLANDS

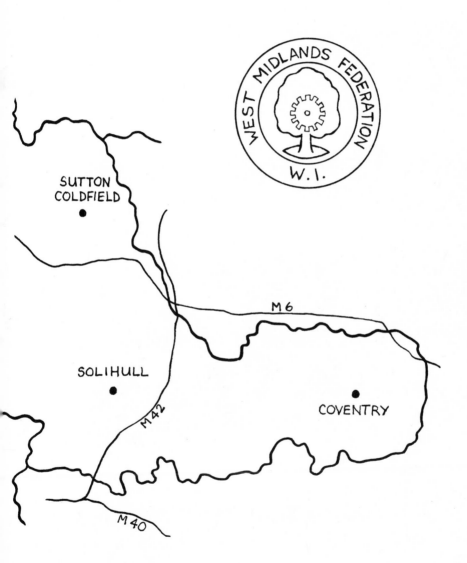

WEST MIDLANDS FEDERATION
W.I.

SUTTON
COLDFIELD

M6

SOLIHULL

M42

COVENTRY

M40

Acknowledgements

The West Midlands Federation of Women's Institutes wish to thank all members and friends who have worked so hard to provide the information and drawings for this book. To Gill Wiley for the map and additional sketches and finally to Innes Brett, the co-ordinator of the project.

Aldridge 🌿

Aldridge, once a village mentioned in the Domesday Book, lies between Walsall and Sutton Coldfield and some nine miles north of Birmingham. In the Domesday Book it was known as 'Alrewych' and at that time was in the Royal Forest of Cannock. It still retains much of a village atmosphere.

The Saxon name meant 'the settlement by the alders' and suggests the presence of water, for these trees cannot survive without it. The natural pools have now all disappeared beneath houses and roads. The area known as Pool Green may have been the centre of the ancient settlement. The narrow, trickling brook which still meanders across the remnant of old meadowland on its north-westward route to the river Tame, ran through that area.

Charcoal-burning, needed for early ironworks, effectively cleared the trees in the area. On the Croft, an oasis of green on which in the past cattle were grazed, facing the parish church of St Mary the Virgin, is an avenue of chestnut trees, as well as a number of other species including a majestic Turkey oak. An ancient mulberry tree stands in the forecourt of the manor house opposite. There is a row of copper beeches in Leighswood Road and a grove of oaks stands in Linley Wood; but where are the alders by which the village was known? Modern drainage has been their downfall.

Romans, who mined the limestone at the opposite end of Aldridge, medieval ironworkers, charcoal-burners and others whose home it was so long ago, like the Stone Age artisans, all left their mark upon local fields. Castlefort on the eastern boundary rears into the sky, raised by Iron Age inhabitants. Farming was once the main occupation of the area, together with mining and brickmaking, the latter still being an important industry as Aldridge is the home of 'etruria marl', from which blue bricks are made and exported all over the world, as well as being used in nearly all the railway bridges in England. Stubbers Green Pools, caused by subsidence, are reminders of the industries of the past. Other present-day industries are on estates at Westgate and Northgate.

Many interesting characters have lived in Aldridge, but none of national note. Some famous people have certainly passed through.

9

John Wesley recalls in his journal about the year 1746 riding on horseback through the wild northern area known as Aldridge Heath. He had been warned of the dangers of crossing it. He wrote, 'Though crusted over completely with snow, I believe we did not go ten yards out of our way'.

Jonathan Swift evidently rode along Chester Road, which lies to the east of Aldridge, passing in sight of the aforementioned Castlefort. One of his poems paints a graphic picture of a stage coach journey on the way to Chester.

During the Civil War King Charles I is said to have reviewed his troops in October 1642 at Kingstanding, which adjoins the southern boundary of Aldridge, and Prince Rupert in the following year seized Rushall Hall near Aldridge for the King, but the Royalists later surrendered to the Earl of Denbigh.

A hero of the First World War, Lieutenant C. G. Bonner VC, DSO, RN, is remembered by a room named in his honour in the community centre and by Bonner Grove on a local housing estate.

To the south and south-east was the area known as the Colefield. Many nefarious activities, including murder, were enacted there, particularly in medieval times. In the first quarter of the 19th century an illegal prize fight took place there and was reported in a broadsheet. It lasted for 213 rounds and attracted a rabble of pickpockets and worse. The gravel pits where events of that nature took place, were still in existence during the first half of this century. They were at the junction of what is now Longwood Road, Barr Common Road and Knight's Hill. The latter was known as Dead Man's Lane, for funeral corteges travelled through it from Great Barr to Aldridge church.

The diminishing green belt area is mainly in the south and east between Birmingham and Walsall. This green belt is marred by two marching lines of electricity pylons. Aldridge once had a railway station with connections between Birmingham, Walsall and Walsall Wood, until the Beeching axe fell upon it in the 1960s. Goods traffic still passes on the line. Travellers today are well served by bus routes to most towns within a radius of 20 miles and can reach Birmingham Airport within an hour.

The parish church is said to have been founded in 1250 by Nicholas de Alrewich, with the tower being built in the 14th century. Its five bells were cast in 1738 by A. Rudhal of Gloucester and the main body of the church was rebuilt in the 1850s. The church, village green, manor house and other properties are covered by a conservation order. The manor house was built in 1851 by Edward Tongue, the last lord of the manor, and for some years prior to 1981 served as the local public library, until a new library was built.

After the rise of Methodism, the villagers built Wesleyan and Primitive Methodist chapels. The two societies later merged and built Wesley Hall in Anchor Road in 1936. Later still the Anglicans opened a small mission church in Tynings Lane and St Thomas's church among new housing at Coppy Hall. The Roman Catholic church of St Mary of the Angels was built in Whetstone Lane. A local ecumenical project is in being between Anglicans and Methodists and an amicable relationship is maintained between all.

Next to the parish church is the Adam-style Moot House, now privately owned but once a school. Also nearby is Aldridge Court, built by an Aldridge man, Frank James, who lived to be 103. It was originally known as Portland House, the name derived from the Portland stone around the windows. It is now a nursing home.

The modern Youth Theatre was opened in 1977 after many years of fund-raising. The cricket and hockey club (the stick and wicket) is situated in Hobs Hole Lane and was founded in 1874. It is very popular with both players and spectators. About one mile from the town centre is a public house called The Old Irish Harp, where it is rumoured that Dick Turpin stayed. The Irish Harp is situated on Chester Road, which linked London and Chester, the journey taking six days by stage coach.

Aldridge's attractions as a residential area are numerous, not the least being its location on the edge of Cannock Chase and the rural Staffordshire countryside. Villagers, as Aldridge folk still call themselves, must still visit nearby towns for some goods, and 'it's not like it used to be' is often said. Those were the days when everyone knew everyone else in the village or was related to them, when the High Street had just a butcher, a baker and a candlestick maker! But there is still plenty of farmland surrounding Aldridge, which makes it a pleasant place to return to after a working day spent in Walsall or Birmingham.

Allesley

In 1140, Ranulf, Earl of Chester was lord of the manor of Awsley – a name derived from Aelfshey, being the old English word for 'a clearing in a wood'. Today the village of Allesley still retains a great deal of its former character as a small medieval village, even though it is only four and a half miles west of Coventry.

In 1968 Allesley was designated as a conservation area and various plaques were placed on buildings in the village to help remind visitors and villagers alike of its historical and architectural interest.

The Rainbow inn at Allesley

Birmingham Road runs through the village and was reconstructed and lowered by Telford between 1825 and 1841. The mail coaches between London, Birmingham and the North all passed through Allesley, and cattle fairs were held regularly on the broad grass verges. Some of the coaching inns can still be seen in the village today, though others have been made into private dwellings. The steps used by visitors to The Rainbow Inn indicate the height of the old road, and at a house opposite the inn there can still be seen a small upstairs window from which the mail-bags were lowered. There is still a gazebo in Rectory Garden, overlooking the Birmingham Road, said to have been used as a 'lookout' for the arrival of the mail coaches, or the carrier's cart.

The aforementioned Earl of Chester requested Bishop Roger of Coventry to allow the building of a chapel for the 'poor people of Allesley' and the present parish church of All Saints stands on the same site today. From 1749 until 1917 the living was held by the Bree family and Mr James Bree still visits and takes a great interest in village activities. The church, which is predominantly of Norman and Early English architecture, is built of red sandstone and is the focal point of village life.

'The Lodge' is a beautiful red brick house, built in 1720 for Christopher Capel, not far from the church. It was used as a curate's residence in the time of the Brees, and was also used as a school at one time. On the opposite side of the road is the popular village inn, The Rainbow, with a timber-framed structure that probably dates from the 16th century, but which was refronted in the 19th century with whitewashed brick.

Not far from The Rainbow is one of the oldest houses in Allesley, The Stone House, reputed to be the original site of the pack-horse gatehouse of the castle (now Allesley Hall). This house is also built of red sandstone and today is owned by Coventry City Council and used as a day centre and luncheon club for the elderly and by the Social Services Training Section.

Before piped water came to the village there were at least two village wells. One was outside Allesley House (now Allesley Hotel) and one near Paybody Hospital (now an eye hospital). The latter used to be a private house called The Elms, then a school, before Thomas Paybody presented it to the Coventry Crippled Children's Guild as a convalescent home. The first 'steam coach' from Coventry to Birmingham used to replenish its water supply from this well and pump, the remains of which can still be seen.

The parish room, now the village hall, which was built in 1898, is another focal point for village activities. Many local organisations use the hall. The WI market sets out its stalls of produce, handicraft and preserves every Wednesday morning and attracts people from far and wide.

There is a Conservation Society which meets once a month in the Bree Room. Originally this was a 'brew house' used for brewing 'hop liquor', but in 1964 it was converted into the present day meeting room by do-it-yourself parishioners. It is a well equipped building owned and hired out by the church, and used by small organisations for meetings.

The church has an octave of bells which ring out every Sunday to beckon people to church. In 1552 there were just three bells in the church tower but by 1750 there were five. The full octave was reached in December 1946. Recently a special celebratory peal of Rutland Surprise Major was rung in honour of the 90th birthday of Allesley's best-known ringer, Mr Hubert Summers.

In 1705, Martha Flynt, widow of Thomas Flynt, lord of the manor, conveyed a cottage and some land adjoining in trust for the benefit of a schoolmaster – the beginning of education in Allesley? There was a school for 'young ladies' and a boarding school for the 'sons of gentlemen' during the first half of the 19th century.

The Victorian village school on the Birmingham Road was opened on 4th May 1874 and the building still stands, though used only as a small library and a play school nowadays. Behind the school the council has used the land to build a complex of sheltered accommodation for the elderly which has been welcomed by the villagers. The new school was built in the early 1960s at Antrim Close.

Under a hedge in one of the fields locally is a lone engraved headstone. It was erected to mark the grave of a pet donkey, belonging to the children of a local farmer. The inscription reads:

'CRAVEN'
Nov. 8th 1899
33 years

The sting in this tale is that although the children must have missed *Craven* greatly, the other residents felt some relief, as the donkey's braying had consistently kept half the village awake at night!

Although Allesley has lost some of the old coaching inns and hostelries, the Allesley Hotel has been enlarged, and the Post House Hotel, and of course the National Exhibition Centre, is not far away and brings considerable business to the village.

Amblecote

The name derives from the Old English 'Aemla's cot', Aemla being a personal name and 'cot', a cottage or shelter for animals.

Amblecote is now a suburb of Stourbridge, a prosperous market town well known for its glass-making. The town has, through the generosity of Andrew Carnegie, the US industrialist born in Scotland, a fine library opened in 1905.

Amblecote, the smallest Urban District in the country, was even more closely linked with Stourbridge because of the Corbett Hospital, which served the whole area. In 1932 Lye, Wollescote and Pedmore were incorporated into the Urban District of Stourbridge, and in 1974 the whole borough was absorbed into the Metropolitan Borough of Dudley in the West Midlands.

In the 17th century the presence of coal and fireclay attracted the attention of glass-makers, particularly those craftsmen who sought refuge in England following persecution in France. These French Protestant Huguenots fled from their homeland in huge numbers and brought with them their many skills, including glass making. When they discovered the fine fireclay in the Stourbridge and Wordesley area, it was here they set up their workshops. This fireclay runs in a belt from Wollescote through Lye, Amblecote, Brierley Hill, Brockmoor to Pensnett and Kingswinford. The clay and coal ran alongside each other and were found to be easily accessible, leading to continued prosperity in the area.

The church of the Holy Trinity was built in the 1840s, when the village was experiencing its period of greatest growth. It is of yellow brick, with a west tower and a wide, aisleless nave. There are a few monuments, including one to the Rev John Crier in 1866 'who died suddenly after preaching in this church'! The 19th century tombs which filled the churchyard to capacity testified to the prosperity of many of those who lived here over a century ago.

The area around Amblecote, today, is still famous, not only for its beautiful glass, but also for the manufacture of large quantities of firebricks, furnace blocks, firebacks and sanitaryware, produced in the many beehive and tunnel-shaped kilns in the Lye area.

Aston ✍

When you travel from the Central Fire Station and speed along the Aston Expressway, a modern straight road, to 'Spaghetti Junction', it is hard to believe you have passed through one of the most historically interesting places in this area.

Estone, or East Farm, (as mentioned in the Domesday Book of 1086) was originally part of the properties belonging to William Fitz-Ansculf, Lord of Dudley. It was more important than the neighbouring village of 'Bermingham' and was worth £5 in annual tax, whereas 'Bermingham' only paid £1. It had a river (the Tame) wandering through a fertile valley, a watermill, a priest, 44 tenants and a total population of 220. It is thought that if only it had had a weekly market, today the city might have been called Aston – not Birmingham.

The parish church of St Peter and St Paul can be seen from the Expressway. Its 200ft high tower and spire contain a full peal of twelve bells. It is a beautiful Gothic church of the 14th to 15th centuries. Its stained glass windows, richly decorated interior, fine organ and many tombstones tell of the prosperity of the area through the ages. This was probably due to Aston having a resident lord of the manor.

Across the road on a hill stands Aston Hall in its own beautiful park, looking down onto the church. This is an early Jacobean house, built in the early 1600s for Sir Thomas Holte, Bart, sheriff of Warwickshire and lord of the manor. It is another fine example of British architecture and built in the traditional shape of the letter E. It took over 17 years to complete and is still very well preserved. It is a magnificent example of Transitional architecture.

The Holte family were true royalists and the manor was given them freehold by Elizabeth I. They accumulated their wealth by selling wool and collecting taxes. They owned it through 14 generations until the line ended in 1782. King Charles I is known to have stayed there during the Civil War. The family looked after the poor and needy of the manor by building almshouses. Eventually in 1858 Aston Hall was opened as a museum by Queen Victoria and the grounds as a public recreation area (Aston Park).

Much work has been done during the last few years on restoring the interior of the house. Tapestries have been re-worked and curtains made to original patterns and colours. Aston Hall can also be seen from the Expressway, on the left hand side, travelling from the city centre. Groups of twisted chimneys and patterned turrets appear above the broken line of gables on the skyline.

The industrial development of Aston started with the building of canals across the area, making transport cheap and easy. The Black Country provided cheap coal and ironstone – and water was readily available. The population grew rapidly. Small home industries, workshops and backyard factories flooded the area as new inventions rapidly took place. Steam started the development of the railway and even more inventions, until by 1887 Aston Manor had several breweries and a distillery. 'Ansells' is still a well known name today, as is HP Sauce. The local well water was found to be particularly suitable for these purposes. Other industries are almost too numerous to mention but include asphalt, coach varnish, soap, glue, buttons, glass, nail and oil works as well as a gun factory, foundry, sawmill and paper mill.

The foundations were laid for the 20th century, which brought the electrical trade (GEC works) in 1901, the rubber trade (Robert Rubber), the chemical trade (ICI Kynoch – later IMI) the cycle (Hercules) and motor trade with all their small components factories. Midland Counties Dairy was also opened, revolutionising the supply of fresh milk to the public.

Aston was still able to look after its residents' recreational needs, and in the 1800s an ornamental park, together with a theatre complex, art gallery, menagerie, aquarium, restaurant and winter-gardens were built, and later a bowling green, sports ground, cycle track and a large indoor skating rink. It was all built near and on what is now known as Aston Villa football ground. Sadly most of the buildings were knocked down to make way for much-needed houses. By 1880 only the present site remained, together with some waste land at the back of the church. Known as the Serpentine, this had been some kind of lake and was filled in with ash. Fairs were held on this land (which is now an Asda supermarket and Aston Villa Sports and Leisure Centre) until quite recently, Pat Collins' Onion Fair keeping just a little of the old tradition going into the mid 1900s. The tall floodlighting pillars of Aston Villa's football ground can also be seen from the Expressway, between the Hall and the church.

Before 1911 Aston had its own Mayor, council houses, police force and fire brigade, but it was impossible for the area to expand. The overcrowding of houses and industries caused the area to become poorer. Birmingham finally took over its finances and Aston became part of Greater Birmingham.

The Second World War brought heavy damage by bombs and land mines aimed at the large factories producing weapons and explosives. Whole streets were wiped out and much rebuilding was necessary after the war. Luckily the Hall and church survived without much damage. High rise blocks of flats were built to rehouse the homeless and to give a more 'open look' to the area. Now hundreds of the small factories have closed down – Ansells has been demolished and larger factories have been closed down or reduced in size, eg GEC. New developments are the Aston Science Park and the university.

Aston University was opened in 1966 and grew out of a former technical college. It is not in the manor – only the north-west end of it is in the parish, but the name is a compliment to Aston's antiquity.

Balsall Common

There is a very interesting map by Christophorus Saxton, dated 1576, depicting 'Parte of Worwickshire' (spelled with an 'o') showing the manor of Balshall when Queen Elizabeth I gave it to

The old wheelwright's shop, Balsall

her favourite, the Earl of Leicester. Balshall is shown as a manor house, and nearby is the hamlet of Barston. A little to the north-east is Berkswell, which merited an appearance in the Domesday Book. To the south is Hunningly and Ketelworth, all names which we can still recognise today.

At that time Balsall stood in the midst of forest and wild heath land. Already, to the west, the Knights Templars had begun to establish themselves and to build. The Saracen's Head in Balsall Street dates back to the 13th century and the time of the Crusades, when the Knights Templars first came here. Today the Saracen's Head is still a flourishing hostelry, and it is a great pleasure to enjoy refreshment there and ponder on its history.

Another very ancient inn still stands to serve the public along

19

the Kenilworth Road. It originally stood by the rough road which was called the 'Welsh Road' and which ran from Wales and the west, then turned south to London. The road across the heath was too wild and dangerous to travel at night, so the inn had large enclosures in which the drovers could keep their cattle safely. When the Hanoverians came to the throne the inn was renamed 'The George'. As at that time the road passed some distance away from the inn, a large board, 'The George', was nailed to a huge elm tree at the side of the road, hence the name – 'The George in the Tree'.

Further along the Kenilworth Road stands the White Horse, now a very imposing establishment, that was once a 'two up and two down' cottage. Here the Balsall Wake was held every August. The women raced from High Cross to the White Horse in an endeavour to win a quarter of tea, and the men bowled for a duck in the field at the back!

The little Tipperary Inn was also a four-roomed cottage and was known locally as the 'Plough', where one of the boundary oaks still stands. It is said that during the First World War, the inn-keeper's crippled son, who was very musical, with the collaboration of a friend, wrote the world-famous *Tipperary*. The new owners have enlarged the premises and renamed it 'The Tipperary Inn'. A plaque has been placed on the wall – 'In memory of Harry Williams of *Tipperary* fame, the world-famous song which helped to save England!' A bold claim!

There were thatched cottages here well into the 20th century. A 16th century cottage stood across the road from where the super-market now stands. It seems the owner was 'advised' to either install modern conveniences or demolish it!

The wheelwright's cottage of about the same vintage still stands in Balsall Street. Here was the centre and heart of the village, a hub of industry at the junction of the road that led up to join the turnpike (Station Road) – the wheelwright, the foundry, the smithy and the sawpit. The cottage today is of course privately occupied.

Further along Balsall Street, standing in a quiet and shady spot, is the delightful St Peter's church. A daughter church of Temple Balsall, it was opened in 1871 and known as Balsall Street chapel. In 1911 it was dedicated to St Peter by Bishop Gore.

Gradually, as the old crafts fell into decline, the centre of village activities moved up towards the junction with the new turnpike road, built along the route of the old Welsh Road. There is an excellent map dated 1875 showing how the parish developed, with new roads across the common and the turnpike through to Kenilworth and beyond, but the whole district was still completely rural, and indeed remained so until the present day.

The modern Balsall Common was almost entirely built during the present century, and until about 100 years ago the village consisted of only a couple of hamlets of six to twelve homes each, apart from a few scattered cottages, the farms, and the landed gentry.

The community today has grown out of all recognition. Its first surge of growth came with the railway and the motor car, which allowed people to work in industrial Coventry and Birmingham but to live in pleasant rural surroundings. Up to the Second World War, however, Balsall Common remained a real village community.

Its life during those dark days of the 1940s is well pictured in *Mrs Milburn's Diary*, a published account of one woman's war. Balsall Common during the blitz became a refuge for the exhausted citizens of Coventry. Night after night they streamed out from the city, and the village hall became an emergency dormitory for the homeless.

With the coming of the 1960s there was a further spurt of building. The old thatched cottages and traditional shops began to disappear, and a new population of young commuters in modern homes took over. Local societies and facilities for children proliferated and the population rose to over 2,500 by the mid-1960s. During this period the village became part of the Metropolitan Borough of Solihull, and the community became more Solihull-orientated.

The latest phase in expansion has taken place over the late 1970s and 1980s. The coming of the National Exhibition Centre, the growth of Birmingham Airport and the improvements in communications through motorways and frequent fast Intercity trains have all had their effect, and the population now stands at over 5,000.

There has always been a little local industry in the village. Old people refer to 'the bedstead factory'. The Arden car was manufactured here in the 1920s, and at present a modern office block houses the national headquarters of an automobile accessories firm. The great majority of wage-earners, however, commute all over the West Midlands, and not a few as far as London and the Home Counties.

Barston

Barston is a small village approximately four miles south of Solihull, formerly in the county of Warwickshire. It was recorded in the Domesday Book of 1086 as Bercestone or Bertonstone.

Evidence of Roman pottery and building has been found near Eastcote, where there could have been a settlement. The shape of the pottery suggests this could belong to the 2nd and 3rd centuries AD.

In the 16th century land was acquired by the Fisher family of Eastcote, and by the 19th century 30 farms were recorded in the area.

This is still an agricultural area, although vastly changed since the Second World War. In 1972 the centre of the village was made a conservation area, and it is of special architectural interest with various types of half-timbered and thatched cottages which date back to the 16th and 17th centuries, one of the thatched cottages being the village shop in the 1900s. As farming has become modernised farmhouses have become private dwellings and many barns have been converted into cottages. However, the village still retains its old world charm.

We once had a village shop and post office, a motor cycle garage and wheelwright's, all family businesses and all sadly closed in recent years.

The church of St Swithin was an ancient chapelry, the register of which dates from 1598, and was annexed to the church of Berkswell, but in 1893 an order was authorised for the separation of the chapelry of Barston. After a fire destroyed this building in 1721 the present church was built and various alterations have been made over the years.

The Church of England school in the village closed in 1944, and

St Swithin's church, Barston

was later sold and converted into a private house. Prior to 1944 one of the highlights of the school calendar was May Day. On the previous evening wild flowers were collected to make garlands for each child to carry in the procession the following day. Starting from the school they walked with a May Queen, singing May Day songs all round the village, ending a busy day dancing round the maypole, with tea in the village hall.

The village still has a coaching inn, where in olden days an ostler tended the horses.

The village hall was originally a malt barn. This was purchased in 1920 by the villagers as a memorial to those who served in the First World War, and named The Memorial Institute.

Two great events were held in 1897. On 4th and 5th June a bazaar, opened by Lady Peel from the manor at Hampton-in-Arden, was very successful. Special arrangements were made with the railway company to issue return tickets at single and a quarter fare on both days, from Birmingham and Coventry to Hampton-in-Arden, and a brake was used to run passengers to Barston for the day. It is recorded that all went very well and a grand total of £242 6s 3d was collected. After expenses, £214 went to the church restoration and organ fund.

On Sunday 20th June 1897 special services were held to commemorate the Diamond Jubilee of Queen Victoria. This was followed on 22nd June with village rejoicings – tea for the children, sports and a bonfire, with supper for all the adults in the parish. The field where all this took place is still known as the 'Jubilee'.

A well known character in the 1930s was Mr Tandy, who delivered milk by horse and float, and served straight from the churn. But on the days when the North Warwickshire hounds held a meet in the village, Bill would finish his early round, return home, saddle up *Peggy* his horse and follow the hunt all day. Returning home later in the afternoon, he would milk the cows, put *Peggy* between the shafts and deliver the afternoon milk! Bill was a very jolly man and always had time for a chat – happy days.

Being a green belt area with strict controls on building and conservation, Barston should remain a very attractive rural village in which to live.

Bentley Heath ❧

The village of Bentley Heath lies two and three quarter miles south of Solihull. The name was first recorded in 1280 and is derived from 'bent grass clearing' or a 'clearing where long coarse grass and rushes grow'. The area was situated in the manor of Longdon and was mainly agricultural, with the local inhabitants having commoner's rights in the heathland. There were two moated sites, Manor Farm in Four Ashes Road, which still exists and where bullrushes can still be found, and Bentley Farm in Mill Lane, where there also stood a sturdy brick towered windmill.

The enclosure of common land in the early 19th century started to change the area and the coming of the Great Western Railway in 1852 accelerated the process. The Drum and Monkey public house is reminiscent of the cut and thrust of the early railway years, being named after the blasting powder carriers, or powder monkeys, and the drums that the powder was stored in. The railway line is still a busy one and Bentley Heath level crossing in Mill Lane is the cause of much discord amongst angry motorists complaining of lengthy waits at the barriers.

Bentley Heath lay in the parish of St Alphege, Solihull, and it was merely regarded as the Widney end of Solihull, but as the population grew in the area, it became clear that the inhabitants needed a church and school of their own. People no longer wished to journey to Knowle or Dorridge on a Sunday and they also wanted a proper school for their children rather than Mrs Knight's school at Tilehouse Farm. Consequently a dual purpose church and school known as the Mission Chapel was built in Widney Road in 1870, a house for the schoolmistress being attached.

The one big schoolroom was divided into two, one half being used to teach the children in and the other half being a chapel dedicated to St Philip and St James. The chapel eventually fell into disuse during the 1960s due to a lack of attendance; this was a blessing in disguise for the teacher using the other half of the room, as she was no longer required to cover up all the secular work on the walls every Friday evening. A new, larger church school built on land next to the old one was opened in 1978 by the Bishop of Birmingham, and was again dedicated to St James, so the long link has been re-established with the old school, which is currently used to teach children with learning difficulties.

Bentley Heath began to be developed in earnest during the 1950s and 1960s and most of the old buildings were swept away in the name of progress, although a few small agricultural and railway workers' cottages remain, together with some imposing Edwardian family homes. The old names linger on however, Red House Close being named after Red House Farm which stood in Widney Road, Widney Free Church being on the site of the old barn and Bentley Farm Close being reminiscent of the farm that once stood in Mill Lane. The only reminder of the old mill however, is the millstone set up in Milton Close.

Berkswell

In Saxon times a tiny clearing in the Forest of Arden, where springs of fresh water flowed, was ruled over by a chieftain, Bercul. It became known as Berculswell. The water from the well, which can still be seen, rises by the church gate and flows into the river Blythe. The river forms the western boundary of the parish and is spanned by a packhorse bridge, which lies on the old salt route from Droitwich to Berkswell.

The highest land in the area forms part of the great watershed of England. Streams to the east flow into the Bristol Channel, via the Avon and Severn, and those to the west flow into the North Sea via the Trent and Humber.

Berkswell church is one of the finest examples of Norman and Early English architecture in the Midlands. The church has a magnificent crypt in which there is some Saxon stonework. The beautiful, and unusual, half-timbered vestry above the entrance

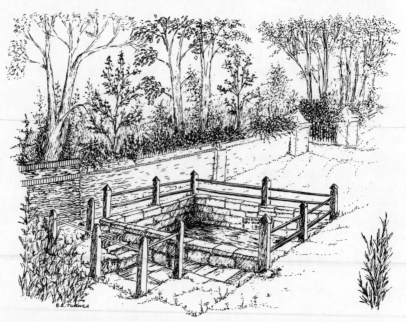

The well, dating back to Saxon times, from which Berkswell village takes its name

porch has been used since at least 1611, for in that year there is a reference in the churchwarden's accounts, 'For amending a steppe of the vestrie stayres'. The key of the vestry, still in use, was made in 1612 at a cost of 4d. There is a fine peal of bells of the 15th and 16th century; in recent years some have been re-cast.

Documentary evidence shows that Oliver Cromwell stationed men and horses in Berkswell before the battle of Kenilworth during the Civil War. Local farmers made claims for damages and for the demands made upon them for fodder. One reads:

> 'Gregory Darby hath suffered in free quarteringe of Captaine Millers soldiers besides the keepinge of the Court of Guards att his house and beinge very unreasonable in their behaviour in his house whilest they tarried there'.

The earliest record of a school in the parish is in 1500. In 1887 each child paid one penny a week to attend school. Maypole dancing is still carried on as it has been for the past 100 years. In recent years the school has been completely modernised, but throughout its history it has remained a Church of England school.

In 1589 'The Church, School and Poorlands Charities' were established after a court case against the lord of the manor. The lands and properties owned by the Charities are still administered, today, by local trustees. This is an entry in the overseer's accounts of 1760:

7th January.	Paid to Widow Fenthem in sickness– one shilling.
22nd June.	Paid to Widow Fenthem in sickness– one shilling.
30th June.	Paid to Widow Fenthem in sickness– one shilling.
5th July.	Paid for eating and drinking at Widow Fenthem's burying – five shillings.

The Berkswell 'Association for the Prosecution of Felons' is one of the oldest in the country. The association was formed because, prior to the establishment of a police force, people were deterred by trouble and expense from prosecuting alleged offenders. A scale of rewards to non-members for the apprehension of persons guilty of certain offences was laid down, ranging from £20 for murder to ten shillings for 'stealing or taking fish in the daytime'. This rose to £1 if the person was apprehended at night.

There is a fine set of stocks on the village green, and also a cattle pound.

During October the 'Stattis' or Statutes Fair was held. This was a hiring fair at which local farmers engaged their servants for the coming year. They met at the Bear Inn. Each man wore, in his smock or hat, the emblem of his trade, a wisp of wool for a shepherd and some horse hair for a waggoner.

On one occasion, believed to be the Diamond Jubilee of Queen Victoria, the black cannon, a prize from the Crimea, and now in front of the Bear Inn, was towed to the top of the hill behind the village, charged with black powder and fired. Windows were broken all over the village and the air filled with partly burned wadding. The 'Stattis' was discontinued at the outbreak of the First World War.

The reading room was opened in 1902 as a meeting place for the 'penny readings' which were a feature of rural life at the end of the 19th century. They were organised by a young curate (believed to have been a nephew of George Eliot) who lodged in the village. The reading room is now used as a village hall.

The windmill stands on high ground in the south of the parish. It is a good example of a typical tower mill. It was in constant use until 1948 and has since been restored.

The Birmingham Museum and Art Gallery has changed little since its extension following a donation of £50,000 in 1905 by Mr John Feeney of Berkswell, the sole proprietor of the provincial newspaper *The Birmingham Post and Mail*. He gave generous endowments to Birmingham University and the General Hospital. He also gave the organ in Berkswell church (a Father Willis organ) and restored the peal of bells.

Miss Maud Watson, daughter of the Reverend Dr Watson, rector of Berkswell, was the first Ladies Lawn Tennis Champion at Wimbledon in 1884. She was the Founder President of Berkswell Women's Institute. Three other ladies, who also held office in the then newly formed Women's Institute were keen supporters of the Suffragette movement before the First World War. They took stones from Berkswell to throw through the windows of No 10 Downing Street and were later imprisoned. During their detention they embroidered their names on the hems of the men's shirts that they were forced to make.

Bilston 🌿

Bilston is about two miles south-east of Wolverhampton. It is an ancient site, mentioned in the Domesday Book, and was a small market town long before the Industrial Revolution. But it has a long industrial pedigree – iron, then steel, manufacture having been carried on here for at least 200 years. In 1790 a visitor to Bilston wrote that 'it is one of the largest villages in England, containing more than 1,000 houses'.

The first mention of the church was made in 1455 when Letters Patent were granted for the 'Dedication of a Chantry to St Leonard'. Several residents made grants of land during the reign of Henry VI for the support of the church, including some 200 acres called Le Prieste Fields – now Priestfield.

The church of St leonard is, said Pevsner, 'the very hub of the town'. There has certainly been a church on this site since medieval times, but the present one was built in 1825–26 by Francis Goodwin. There are some interesting memorials, including one to Mary Pearce, who died in 1836 and claimed descent from 'three children of King Edward the First'.

The curfew bell was rung regularly from early times to the middle of the 19th century. According to a law introduced by William the Conqueror, a bell was to be rung in summer at sunset and at 8 o'clock in winter, when all fires and lights had to be extinguished. On one of the old Bilston bells was the inscription –

> 'I am called ye Curfewe belle
> I ryngen att VIII or more
> Too sende ye alle too bedde
> And waken ye up att IV'

The ringer of the 8 pm bell was paid 15 shillings per quarter.

The establishment of organised Noncomformity in the town dated back to 1775. The first chapel was in a street called Meeting Street, founded by a body called the Independents.

Industry of course, often brought squalor and disease in its wake. In 1832 an outbreak of cholera killed 742 people in six weeks. A national appeal for help for Bilston raised some £8,000, and a quarter of that went towards a school for 450 orphans. However, little seems to have been learned, for in 1847 another outbreak took 730 lives. There is an area by the Penn Road where the corpses of those who died are said to have been flung into quicklime – not unnaturally there are also tales of ghostly cries and apparitions.

After coal and iron were found in the district, the forging of weapons and tools became a local art. Grindstone is a natural product of the area and this has led to the production of both natural and artificial abrasives, grinding wheels and grinding apparatus.

John Wilkinson was born in 1728 at Bradley. A commemorative plaque erected in Great Bridge Playing Fields (now in Walsall) by the Bilston Historical Society in 1956, recorded that Wilkinson erected the first Black Country blast furnace nearby in 1757–8. It was certainly worthy of commemoration, for this was the 'mother furnace' of the Black Country. The blast was created by leather bellows, but later Wilkinson and the Darbys of Coalbrookdale were the first ironmasters to adopt the use of an engine to provide the blast, which was needed for melting the ore. Wilkinson went on to make his fortune. He was buried, as he had requested, in an iron coffin!

In 1862 Sir Henry Newbolt was born here at the vicarage (since demolished). Sir Henry is perhaps best remembered for his sea songs, including *Drake's Drum*, and for the archetypal Victorian exhortation to 'Play up! play up! and play the game!'

In the Middle Ages, in common with many other towns and villages, Bilston people held an annual Watch Service in honour of St Leonard, their patron saint. His feast day was November 6th, and on the night before the parishioners would carry lighted candles into the churchyard, there to keep watch over their dead. The custom was called 'waking' or 'the Wakes', derived from an Anglo-Saxon word meaning 'to keep a vigil'. After the Reformation the custom lost its religious significance and became merely an excuse for a holiday. The Wakes festivities would last several days. In 1930 the Bilston Carnival, held in June, was begun to keep alive the spirit of the old Wakes custom.

Bilston still has something of the aura of a village, despite its modern expansion. It has its own museum, Bilston people having a great, and justifiable, pride in their past. There are still some unspoilt 19th century houses and shops, and St Leonard's still exerts a peaceful influence.

Bloxwich 🌿

Bloc's village was part of the Anglo-Saxon kingdom of Mercia and it was mentioned in the Domesday Book in 1086. It is now a northern suburb of Walsall.

In 1338 Sir Thomas le Rous sold his share of the manor of Walshale to Sir Ralph Bassett. His son married Joanna, daughter of Thomas Beauchamp, Earl of Warwick. He died childless and his manor passed to the Warwick family, whose emblem – the Bear and Ragged Staff – was adopted by Walsall Borough as its Coat of Arms.

The Black Death, bubonic plague, which had spread from the Far East, reached the area in 1349. The effect was to devastate the whole area and recovery was slow.

The oldest monument in Bloxwich is the preaching cross in the churchyard, thought to date from the 13th or 14th century. The church itself was originally dedicated to St Thomas of Canterbury, but was re-dedicated and the name changed to 'All Saints' in 1875, when the foundation stone to the tower was laid.

The first inn recorded in Bloxwich was the sign of the Talbot. The sign would be a large hunting dog, and refers to the Earl of Shrewsbury.

For many years the area was well known for flax growing. The cultivation of flax and hemp was very important in Tudor times.

During the Civil War much of this area was fought over. Colonel Fox captured Stourton Castle on 30th May 1644 and thus enabled the Parliamentary Forces to reduce the Royalist garrisons in Warwickshire and Worcestershire.

There seems to be one sole reference to the building of the canal which was to have such a far reaching effect upon the area. 'In 1794 the Birmingham Canal Company obtained new powers by which they were enabled to extend their canal from Wednesbury to Walsall – a branch of four and a half miles in length. The Wyley and Essington Canal was projected in 1792 and the branch from

Bloxwich to the Birchills was constructed at this time. The extension Act from Birchills to Pelsall was obtained in 1794'.

Economically the construction of the canal did much for the town. It was now possible to export coal and limestone from Bloxwich. This, in its turn, brought prosperity and increased trade and productivity to the 'Bloxwich Bitties', locksmiths and tackies, the makers of fine leather goods and saddlery at Little Bloxwich and Great Bloxwich.

This development was as important to the Bloxwich area as the invention of the great steam engines was to other parts of the Midlands.

The Wyley and Essington Canal was constructed in such a way that it made the connection between the two great canal systems, thus enabling the goods from Bloxwich to be moved quickly and easily to both London and Liverpool.

Walsall was first served by a railway when the Grand Junction Railway was opened from Birmingham to join up with the Liverpool and Manchester line. By 4th July 1837 the line was complete. Thus Bloxwich became connected by the great transport systems of road, rail and canal to neighbouring towns and villages and to the great ports of the British Isles and to the ships which carried Bloxwich goods to all parts of the world.

Bournville 🌿

Bournville, which rightly occupies a position of major importance in the development of the model estate and garden village, began when, in 1878, the brothers George and Richard Cadbury, took the decision to move their cocoa and chocolate factory out of Birmingham into the countryside. In the June of that year they bought 14½ acres of land at Bournbrook, a rural area some four miles to the south-west of the city.

The two brothers were considered by the business world in Birmingham to be taking a risk in moving away from their sources of labour and ease of supply of raw materials, but the site of the new factory was astutely chosen, for two lines of communication bounded it; the Worcester-Birmingham Canal and the West Suburban Railway. Both were immediately useful, for materials for the factory were brought out by canal and special workmen's fares negotiated with the railway company, enabling the workforce to travel out to Bournbrook. The Cadburys were not the first to move a business from town to country, for Sir Titus Salt had already done so in the 1850s when he founded Saltaire, near Bradford.

The new Cadbury factory was built in 1879 and by the October of that year 14 cottages for the foremen and a house for the works manager were begun. They were completed in May 1880. None of these early houses now survive; built close to the factory, their sites were gradually taken by it.

For a small number of people, however, these first years provided the rural home which was George Cadbury's ideal for working class housing, and which his biographer, A. G. Gardiner, suggested in 1923, may have originated in his liking for staying occasionally in a small cottage at Bittell Reservoir, in Worcestershire. Certainly George Cadbury saw in the rural existence a healthy alternative to the crowded, insanitary conditions in which most of his workforce lived. Both the brothers were ardent members of the Society of Friends and saw the move out to the country as being part of an improvement of the quality of life.

By the end of 1879 the name Bournville had been adopted rather than the original Bournbrook. It had a more commercial French sound to it, for in those days French chocolate was esteemed as better than British. A Society of Friends meeting was begun at the factory in 1882, and in 1885 twelve cottages, which survive, were built by George Cadbury in nearby Stirchley, joined in 1891 by an Institute which housed a Friends Meeting House. In the same year a further Institute and six cottages were begun on land at Northfield, further to the south-west.

The influence of the Institutes was great; they were open to anyone and provided schools for both adult and child education, places for innocent social amusement such as billiards or skittles and, since one of the Friends' ideals was temperance, coffee houses. Provisions against the sale of alcohol were included in the deeds of trust of Northfield Institute and of the later Bournville Village Trust of 1900. Furthermore, the Northfield cottages had large gardens, indicative of what was to follow at Bournville.

Bournville proper was begun in 1895 after the purchase of

further land to the west and north of the orginal site. George Cadbury (and it was he who fostered the village from then on), set up a Building Estate, independent of the factory, and issued a pamphlet stating its aims. The plots of land were to be let on leases of 999 years, leasing, Cadbury felt, being necessary to maintain the rural quality of the area. No house was to be below a certain size and none were to cost less than £150 to construct. Mortgages at 2½% were offered to those who made a 50% deposit at the outset. The aim was to attract the sort of working man who could save.

The lessees very often commissioned the houses in the early days, although the first houses of 1895, three semi-detached pairs in Maryvale Road, were commissioned by George Cadbury. Their architect was Alfred Walker and apart from the new Estate Office in Bournville Lane, these are his only buildings in the village. By December 1895 the work of designing houses had been taken over by a remarkable man, William Alexander Harvey, who was only 20 years of age, and he more than any other architect gave Bournville its characteristic appearance.

Harvey came from an artistic background, his father and brother both being stained glass painters. His architecture has its basis most of all in the principles of the Arts and Crafts movement, with its emphasis upon good materials and sound construction, in addition to which he was influenced by the forms of local earlier vernacular buildings, such as farms and cottages.

Harvey's houses (and he was the designer of most in Bournville from 1896 to 1904) stand easily in their landscape, and because not every consecutive building plot in each road was always built upon at once, there are houses of differing dates side by side in most roads. What appears to be a picturesque mixing of ideas and motifs is the result of changes in the architect's style over the years. Sites on which Harvey had not built were later filled by the equally interesting cottage-style houses of his successor as Estate Architect, Henry Bedford Tylor.

Harvey's style can range from the elegantly simple cottage to quite elaborate compositions with wide-spreading eaves, buttresses and half-timbering, but his detailing usually has a practical purpose. The wide eaves that change their angle of slope lower down, for example, function to lessen the impact of rain. Half-timbering becomes increasingly used only where a whole structure

34

such as a bay window could be built of it; he was well aware of the problems it could cause if used only for decoration in a wall. He came to prefer brindled Staffordshire brick with its hard, durable surface and varied colours for his houses and often used differing tiles, clay, pantiles or slates on adjoining house blocks to create visual interest. His houses of 1906–10 on the development called the Bournville Tenants' Estate, further south-west from the village centre, and his impressive public buildings for the village, such as the meeting house and the schools, show his style at its most developed. He also, before the First World War, supervised the reconstruction in the village of the largely medieval Selly Manor, which originally stood about a mile away.

All the houses had large gardens and residents were encouraged to grow their own vegetables and fruit, each garden being supplied with eight apple and pear trees. The growth of these trees, the planting of trees along the roads and preservation of existing trees wherever possible, gave Bournville its well tree'd appearance even by the time of the First World War.

By that date the village had been run by its own Trust since 1900, and astonishingly enough, only 35 years had gone by since the first houses were built in what was then open country. Within a few years of its foundation, there were parks and open spaces, a row of shops, the schools, an Arts and Crafts Institute, and places of worship providing for a true community in ways previously unheard of, which were to become the model for those who came after.

In the early part of the 1950s, with the rapid expansion of the West Midlands and the urgent demand in the region for additional housing, the Trust decided to embark on the largest, single development scheme since its foundation, in conjunction with the City.

This scheme consisted of 580 dwellings, with community facilities. Higher housing densities demanded by the planners meant much more intensive use of the land available, and this was achieved by introducing blocks of three-storey flats into the layout. During the 1960s and the 1970s work took place on other parts of the Estate.

In 1967, the Government passed the Leasehold Reform Act, enabling leaseholders to purchase their freehold after a qualifying period of residence. In order to protect the amenity of the Estate, and so that the Trust could retain a measure of control over the development in the future, a Scheme of Management was obtained from the High Court, in 1972.

The Estate today comprises over 7,500 dwellings of different types and sizes, ranging from one bedroom bungalows to five bedroom detatched houses with large gardens. There are maisonettes, flats, terraced and sémi-detached houses as well as shops, schools, churches and a whole range of community buildings. In today's terms, it is a far cry from the original Building Estate of 1895 with its 143 leased cottages.

In the 1930s the Trust acquired 2,700 acres of agricultural land consisting of some woodland, farm land and open spaces, most of which is leased for agricultural purposes or open to the public in some form or another.

Brierley Hill & Kingswinford 🐝

Brierley Hill is about two miles south-west of Dudley. It is truly on a hill, with views towards Dudley and its castle, to Netherton, Birmingham, and to the Clent Hills and the countryside beyond. There has been a settlement on the 'hill where the briars grow' since Roman times. There are the remains of a small Roman camp on Ashwood Heath. The area was later settled by Britons, who in their turn, were driven out by Saxon invaders in the 5th century. It was these Saxon settlers who gave the hill its name.

The hunting grounds of the Earls of Mercia and later kings, stretched away to the river Severn beyond the Smestow Stream and by Kinver Forest.

In the month of November 1605, when the Gunpowder Plot against King and Parliament was discovered, two of the plotters, Robert Catesby and Thomas Percy, fled to nearby Holbeche House, on the road from Himley to Stourbridge. They were caught there and shot dead by the Sheriff of Worcestershire's men, supposedly as they tried to give themselves up.

On what was then wild common land in the parish of Kingswinford, squatters began to work the local resources. Brierley Hill was very much a creation of the Industrial Revolution, and soon furnaces, forges and brick kilns, as well as coal pits, were appearing, to lay the foundations of today's iron and glass works. Royal Brierley Crystal are only one of the world famous lead crystal glassware producers in the area today.

It was early in the 17th century that the glassmakers settled in the area attracted by the coal and brick-clay. The first glassmakers headed their bills 'Stourbridge'. Today all 'Stourbridge Glass' is actually made in the districts of Wordsley, Brierley Hill and nearby Amblecote.

Another early and important industry of the Brierley Hill area was fireclay mining and the manufacture of glass-house pots, firebricks, furnace linings and, later, retorts. The products from this glass-house pot clay were sent all over the country in the 17th century and all over the world in the 18th.

The new means of transport – canals and later, railways – which were being developed meant that goods could move more easily to all parts of the country. Over the years the roads, which were never much more than tracks, had been worn into pot-holes and ridges, and had become wholly unsuitable for wheeled vehicles, particularly for the transport of such fragile goods as glass.

One of the smaller industries which became established in the area was chain making. There were nailers and chain makers at Quarry Bank. Chain making was a domestic industry. The work was carried out in 'shops' around the hovels where the nailers lived. The whole family was involved in the industry, even the very young children. They all worked six days a week and very long hours for just a few shillings. Normally wages were not paid in cash, but in kind from the 'tommy shops' of the middle man or 'Fogger'. He was, very often, also the landlord who supplied the iron and received the finished chains at his warehouse. The workers were exploited and life was hard and grim.

Brierley Hill also became world famous for such diverse products as heavy industry, knitwear, ornamental iron work, and ham and bacon curing.

The church of St Michael was built in 1765, of brick, and the west tower was restored and the church largely rebuilt, in 1900. One of the stained glass windows was given by John Corbett, the 'Salt King' of Droitwich, who is buried in the churchyard.

Delph Locks is a well known attraction. Still known locally as 'Ninelocks' even though there are only eight, the flight of locks climbs the hill towards Dudley. Horses were of course used to tow the barges, and half way up the hill can be seen some old stables.

Brierley Hill is still at the heart of a local community. A new shopping development at the Moor Centre was opened in the 1980s.

Kingswinford, which became part of the Urban District of Brierley Hill in 1934, was, unlike its neighbour, an ancient place of settlement. It lies on one of the saltways radiating out from Droitwich, and the name appears to be derived from 'the ford for the king's swine'. In St Mary's church, itself a product of Georgian or early Victorian times, there is a Norman tympanum of St Michael and the dragon. Kingswinford today is a pleasant residential suburb, close to the Shropshire countryside.

Brownhills 🌿

Brownhills is now a largely residential suburb of Walsall. The name of Brownhills comes from the 'red marls', a geological feature of the area.

Much of the area was once either agricultural land or 'waste' at the edge of Cannock Chase, but coal and clay deposits discovered in the district ensured that Brownhills, on the edge of the Black Country, grew into a sizeable industrial town in the 19th century. Originally a mining community, it remained so until well into this century.

The coming of the canals opened up the region and carried a great deal of traffic as the mining industry flourished.

St James' church was built in 1850. There is some Art Nouveau glass in the west window.

Burton Green 🌿

Burton Green is a quiet village situated in an elevated position in the green belt on the edge of the industrial city of Coventry.

In about 1500 the boundary between Warwickshire and Berkswell ran down the middle of Cromwell Lane, one of the village's main roads. This line of demarcation still exists so that the services (refuse collection, water, electricity, etc) of this tiny village are administered by different authorities, now Solihull District Council, Warwick District Council and Coventry City Council.

The population has grown gradually since the Second World War. Some of the older residents temporarily sheltered in the village during the bombing of Coventry and later put down roots here. Since then the pattern has been to build larger, more expensive houses for professional people attracted to the village because it is within easy access of towns and cities of the region but is still in a pleasant rural setting.

A railway used to run non-stop through the village, from Balsall Common to Leamington. The disused railway track which bisects the village affords elevated panoramic views of the surrounding countryside, and provides an area of interest and beauty where flora and fauna (including rare wild orchids) are preserved.

The whole area around the village has an extremely high water table and even in drought conditions, water can be found less than one metre from the surface of the ground. In fact, the field at the confluence of the three lanes is the last and final outcrop of the Pennine Chain, the main watershed of England that runs on a north-south escarpment and determines the weather on both the western and eastern sides of England. This field is visibly humped or curved, one side draining down to the Wash and the other to the Bristol Channel.

Burton Green Church of England primary school is unusual on two counts. Although the bulk of the site stands in the parish of St Nicholas' church, Kenilworth, the peculiar boundary arrangements which affect the village are also evident here, as children on opposite sides of the playground stand in Berkswell parish and Kenilworth parish respectively.

Secondly, the school was built in 1875, both as an educational institution and as a chapel of ease. In days when horseback was the fastest mode of transport, the building made it easier for the villagers to attend a church. Therefore services have been held at the school for over a hundred years, and are still held monthly.

The water tower in Cromwell Lane dominates the landscape and can be seen from miles around. It is known as the Tile Hill Water Tower and was built in 1932 by a German firm, strangely enough escaping damage during the bombing of Coventry. Access to the tank and roof is by a spiral staircase which passes in a tube through the centre of the tank. The tower is used to serve the local area with water, but its main use is to hold water at a high level (above the roofs of the houses) so that there is a good 'head' of water flowing in the pipes serving Coventry.

Red Lane Reservoir was built in 1966 and is situated on the west side of Red Lane near Burton Green. Inside a fenced enclosure stands a reinforced concrete, rectangular, semi-sunk reservoir which has grassed-over banks and roof. This underground reservoir is capable of supplying Kenilworth and Warwick.

In the fields which now belong to the electricity sub-station can be found five or six circles, about nine feet in diameter and 20 yards apart, which have darker coloured soil than the surrounding area. This is where local people covered the wood they had gathered with clay etc and then burned it slowly in order to produce charcoal. The circles can be easily identified because the grasses and plants growing on these charcoal rings are visibly taller than the rest.

On a map of the area c1500, at present in the Warwick archives, the road from outside the school to the top of Red Lane is not called Hob Lane but 'Dirty Gap'. One local historian claims that the name derives from a time when trees were being felled and taken to a tannery at the bottom of Red Lane, where their bark was used to produce dyes. The logs were dragged by six horses, resulting in the road becoming churned up and muddy and thus called 'Dirty Gap'.

The area next to the Massey Ferguson factory is where Oliver Cromwell gathered his troops as he prepared an assault on Kenilworth Castle during the Civil War. Here his army raised its banners and the road has been called Banner Lane ever since.

Cromwell led his men from their assembly point and up the lane which now bears his name. When his soldiers turned left into the cart track which led to Kenilworth Castle they encountered a skirmish party of Royalist troops. It is said that a fierce battle ensued with many wounded and killed and the place ran red with blood, providing the cart track with the name it has since been known by – Red Lane.

However, a more practical, but less romantic, explanation for the name is offered by studying the physical geography of the area, which appears to be rich in red clay. In fact the redness of the soil is not clay at all but rotted Midland red sandstone, which is the material that has been used for centuries to build many public buildings, including Coventry Council House and the old Coventry Cathedral.

The pound by the railway bridge in Cromwell Lane is where animals used to be kept and at its centre was the old village well, which was 120 ft deep. It was only covered with boards until 1975, when a six-inch thick slab or 'raft' of concrete was placed over the well to prevent accidents.

When King George V and Queen Mary visited Coventry they would stay aboard the royal train overnight in the railway cutting with policemen guarding all the bridges. It was a common sight to see the Royal couple walking along the banks in the morning, collecting primroses and other wild flowers.

The confluence of Cromwell Lane, Hob Lane and Red Lane was a point on the old cattle droving road from the Welsh hills to London. The cattle had usually been on the hoof for some days before they reached the fields near the end of Windmill Lane. Here they were rested in order to feed and gain in weight and strength for the remainder of the journey. After three or four days in which to recover the cattle often became very lively and frisky and their drovers had great difficulty in catching them. That particular resting place thus became known as 'Catchems Corner'.

In the 1930s it was a long straggling village. There were single houses, semi-detached bungalows and groups of houses, with many gaps between which, since the Second World War, have been filled in. There were no footpaths and no street lighting, two shops, a public house and a school.

The Peeping Tom pub started as a cottage and was originally a free house until the breweries took it over. In the early days of the 'Tom', a Mr Docker who had a fishmonger's stall in Coventry Fish Market would bring his unsold fish to the pub and sell it off – there were no refrigerators in those days!

The property known as The Hollies was built in 1858 to replace three cottages in the adjoining fields. As they were part of the Stoneleigh estate, they were built to the design of the then Lady Leigh. During the Second World War, 'Seatons' field was the site for many caravans for folk who had been bombed out of Coventry,

41

either as permanent living quarters, or just as a safe dormitory away from the city.

The village hall in Hodgetts Lane was built in 1923, on land given by a Miss Palmer of a local farming family. It was used for all the village activities until 1982, when a new hall was built at the rear – the site of the old hall is now the car park.

During the late 1950s and early 1960s, a resident in one of the cottages in Hob Lane, being a railway buff, laid down a narrow gauge railway complete with station, and occasionally held open days for charity. When he left the area, the line was lifted and the locomotive, *The Doll*, was given to a steam railway preservation society.

After the Second World War, car production in Coventry rocketed and space was needed to store cars and tractors, the latter coming from Massey Ferguson, Broad Lane, and cars from Standard Motor Works in Canley. A large proportion were stored behind the school, being taken by Canley Car Delivery Services.

In the early 1950s, a local farmer, Mr R. Mackay, sold several acres of land to the local Electricity Board – this became the sports ground with access in Cromwell Lane.

In conclusion, Burton Green has reverted to its state of semi-isolation, due to the closure of shops and deterioration of public transport, but still retains its inherent individuality.

Castle Bromwich 🎔

Castle Bromwich is situated about five miles to the east of Birmingham. It is not mentioned in the Domesday Book but is mentioned in a document in 1168 as Bramwice.

There had been a settlement on the site since prehistoric times; Stone Age implements and ancient ditches were uncovered by archaeologists in 1969, alongside evidence that Roman, Saxon and Norman peoples had settled on this elevated area of land close to a natural ford across the river Tame. The ancient Chester Road, the 'Ridgeway', was cut across the densely wooded Arden Forest in the 13th century, bringing more travellers and settlers to the area. As the village grew it became known by several names – Bramewice, Bromwych, Castelbromwic – each name reflecting the

Church of St Mary and St Margaret, Castle Bromwich

old word 'brom' for the yellow flowering broom which still grows profusely in the area.

'Castle' was added to its name in the 13th century in order to distinguish it from Little Bromwich and Wood Bromwich (long since disappeared). The castle itself was on a hill north of the church. It was never a stone or brick building but was of the motte and bailey type with defensive earthworks, moats and wooden stockades.

In the 16th century Sir Edward Devereaux, the first MP for Tamworth, was responsible for building Castle Bromwich Hall. It was originally a simple single-storey building, that was later bought and extended by the wealthy Bridgeman family. In 1792 they were created Barons of Bradford and during their ownership of the Hall, a marriage in the family brought the Newport estate (Weston Park) into their possession. Today descendants of this family still reside at Weston Park and they have given permission for the Castle Bromwich Gardens Trust to be set up to recreate the gardens and holly hedge maze, which was laid out to the same plan as the maze at Hampton Court. The Orangery too is being restored, using bricks specially handmade in Suffolk, and sand-

43

stone quarried in Staffordshire. The roof will be glazed to allow citrus trees to be over-wintered as they were in the 18th century.

These Earls of Bradford were very wealthy. They leased out farmland and owned the cottages of those who worked on their estates, and with this hereditary power they controlled the community of Castle Bromwich through the land, the farms, the church and the school. As recently as 1902 this power remained in evidence; following complaints about drunkenness in the village, the Earl decreed that The Bradford Arms should be closed and The Castle Inn cease to be a licensed house. He did, though, buy the Castle Inn and controlled its licensing hours, closing it all day on Sundays.

Most of the Bradford land was sold for building in the 1930s. After the Second World War the Hall was leased to GEC and subsequently was left empty for some years. It now belongs to a construction company, which has taken a great deal of trouble in restoring the house for its headquarters.

There is some evidence that a small chapel stood on the site of the present church as early as 1175. This was probably a wooden building. It was replaced in the 15th century by a large half-timbered structure, built using roughly cut oak timber from the forest of Arden. In the 16th century it was enlarged and a bell turret added.

In the 18th century Lord Bradford commissioned Thomas White to build a new church. He did this by encasing the nave and pillars supporting the roof and making a new ceiling below the medieval roof. The impressive old beams can still be seen inside the roof.

The church is dedicated to St Mary and St Margaret and is brick-built with a west tower. To all intents and purposes it is a Georgian church. Prior to 1894, the church was a chapel of ease belonging to Aston church. Baptisms and burials could take place there, but marriages had to be performed in Aston, about four miles away.

During the 18th century, Castle Bromwich was a fairly important place as it was at the junction of two turnpike roads. The main one, the Chester Road, going from London to Chester, joined the Birmingham to Coleshill road near Castle Bromwich Hall. There was a toll gate near the green and several coaching inns. One of these was the Bradford Arms, which is still in use and has stable blocks in its courtyard. Apart from the turnpike roads, most local roads were probably cart tracks connecting up the farms and settlements.

In the 1840s, the peace of the village was disturbed by the arrival of the railway navvies as they built the Birmingham and Derby Junction railway. The Earl of Bradford informed the railway company that he wished a station to be built at Castle Bromwich but sold the land on condition that no trains would call on Sundays! Castle Bromwich station was closed during the 1960s and has since disappeared.

Until 1931 Castle Bromwich had an area of 2,700 acres but in that year the City of Birmingham 'gobbled up' over half of it, leaving only about 1,200 acres. The population had been decreasing since 1841, when 779 people lived in Castle Bromwich. In 1981, in an area less than half of that in 1841, the population was 10,742. The reasons for these vast changes were threefold. Until the 1920s Castle Bromwich was almost entirely agricultural. In 1851 three quarters of the men were directly concerned with agriculture. Agricultural wages were poor and there was a gradual drift into Birmingham where there was work in the new factories. Then, as transport improved in the 1920s, and as the better off factory owners and managers wished to move to more salubrious surroundings, Castle Bromwich became a desirable place to live and a few larger houses were built. In the 1930s there was a great rash of house building, as the large estates began to be sold off. More houses were built in the 1950s and many more in the 1980s when the last farmland was sold.

Today Castle Bromwich is a suburb of Birmingham but it still clings to its rural background. It has two open greens, one with its own WI, Whateley Green. There is still the wide avenue of horse chestnut trees planted a hundred years ago to give a long leafy approach to the Hall. Some old cottages remain, as does the board school, village store, malt house and The Bradford Arms – all echoes of a long and ancient past.

Catherine-de-Barnes 🦢

Before and during William the Conqueror's reign, the lands here were held by one Almar for Turchil de Warwick – part of the manor of Longdone. From 1100, during the reign of Henry I, the area was owned by Chetelberne or Ketelbarnus, who gave land on which to build a nunnery in the Henwood Lane area, then called Estwell.

The nunnery was dedicated to St Margaret and the Benedictine nuns were given all tithes within the precinct of Solihull by Pope Gregory IV. Afterwards the name of Estwell was discarded and the nunnery was called Heanwood.

By 1389 it was a house of about 56 nuns, the reigning monarch still being benefactor of the nunnery. As time passed however, the number of nuns dwindled to twelve.

Henry VIII dissolved Heanwood as he did other monasteries and convents. What became of the poor creatures whose only known home was ruthlessly taken from them, we shall never know. The prioress, however, was granted a retirement annuity of £3 6s 8d. Thus passed Heanwood nunnery, leaving us with Henwood Lane as a memorial.

Catherine-de-Barnes was not a parish in its own right as it did not have a parish church, and therefore it appears only in the records of Hampton-in-Arden. Different names have been given over the years to this lovely little place. Catherine-de-Barnes was, in 1602, Katherine-A-Barnes Heath, then Ketelburn Heath, Catley and Catley Barnes! For at least the past 65 years or so however, it has been Catherine-de-Barnes!

The building of the canal must have been the great awakening. After the survey was passed in 1793 the Warwick and Birmingham Canal was started. It began at Digbeth and the line opened in 1799. Surveyors, engineers, planners, foremen and navvies came to Catherine-de-Barnes and, of course, the Boat Inn – very necessary for the refreshment of all. The fun and fights that issued from the hostelry must have given the villagers a taste of life not known before.

The next notable event in the village, obviously now grown in the number of inhabitants, was in 1880 when a small church and school was opened in Hampton Lane by a Mr J. Gillot of Berry Hall, Solihull. It is still the local school and it and the church are still in full use, many organisations making use of the excellent facilities.

In the early 1900s all infectious fevers, typhoid, cholera, scarlet fever and smallpox were treated in one wing of Olton Hospital – now disappeared without trace. After much wrangling, Yardley, Meriden and Solihull opted out of the Olton Group and corrugated iron huts at Marston Green were surrounded with barbed wire and declared to be the local smallpox hospital. Eventually Yardley withdrew and then Meriden, leaving Solihull to soldier on alone. An alternative site was selected in Henwood Lane. A splendid isolation hospital, brick built, was erected and opened in 1910 and, with the closure of Olton Hospital, became the only smallpox hospital this side of Birmingham. Later, perhaps during the Second World War, it was used as a maternity hospital and afterwards was not in use until 1966. It was then opened again and kept ready for emergencies. The last patients were admitted in 1978.

Cheswick Green 🌿

Between the Blythe and the Stratford Road, south of The Mount, lies water meadow, damp, even flooded seasonally, and unremitting Midland clay, natural land for willow and good summer grazing. Once that was its sole purpose – summer grazing for Brailles, a village of the south of the county of Warwick. For centuries the folks hereabout wanted no more than reasonable grazing and ozier for baskets. So the meadows served their purpose.

The Domesday Book comments as follows: 'Land for one plough. There is a priest. One villein with two bordars. A plough and mill worth three shillings and three acres of meadow. It was worth five shillings and is worth ten shillings.'

But it is the Blythe which made the water meadow and the good grazing, which brought the cattle from Brailles, and which in turn gave rise to the name 'Cheswick' – 'ches' which is cheese and 'wick' a holding, farm or place. In early summer, when the milk yield is at its height, it would not last a journey home, so it was used to make cheese. Even today there is a local cheese-maker, just down the road and second to none.

Cheswick Green is now in West Midlands, but once it was part of Warwickshire, in the parish of Tanworth in Arden. There may have been an outlying farmhouse here then, possibly moated. In 1267 it is recorded that William of Ulnhall (Ullenhall is now a village between Henley in Arden and Tanworth) held this land. Thirteen years later Richard Quenild (Creynolds Lane now bounds the village to the south-east) acquired land 'opposite Cheeswych' for one halfpenny per annum. From those earliest times when the Mount, now a patch of rough coppice and romantic memory, was used to defend peaceful herders and their charges against the lawlessness of the Middle Ages, the holding passed by marriage and sale amongst the great families emerging in the area. Their names are still here, Henry de Sydenhalle (Sidenhales Farm), and John Waring (Warings Green Farm) who bought Cheswick in 1368. Eventually Cheswick passed to the Crewenhalle family, who held it through five generations, passing at last as marriage portion to William Parker of Chartley, who married a Crewenhalle daughter.

Lack of other news suggests the land was peaceably and quietly enjoyed down the years to 1737, when it was sold to John Dawes. Then nothing noteworthy arises, not even the regular flooding of the water meadows, until the 20th century.

Around 1905 Philip Baker, a solicitor from Birmingham, restored the idea of Cheswick Green as a summer place, a pleasure ground, an escape from busy, grubby 'Brum'. He bought Bannister and Mount Dairy Farms, had a refreshment room and a ballroom built, and constructed tennis courts and a bowling green. It is said a troupe of pierrots performed there in the open air. Donkey rides were available (for a fee) all along the Donkey Drive, a path once linking Tanworth Lane and the Stratford Road, part of which is now Boscobel Road. Commercially this early 'theme park' did not prosper. The First World War finished it off, although some functions did take place later. As a whole the area was parcelled off into plots, about 2,000 yards at £75 for the freehold, five shillings extra for every established apple tree.

The sites were used for weekend cottages, but more allotment-and-shed than 'Homes and Gardens'. The authorities did not approve, as sanitation had been insufficiently considered. Then came the Second World War. Bombed out of Birmingham, or fearful for wives and children, families moved to the gimcrack little houses, while others came for weekends only to 'Dig for Victory'. Mr Bond, who now owned the area, even moved his factory here. It made bakelite, a precursor of modern plastic.

After the war, large parts of the village became rather bitty with weekenders and holiday folk, while farmers struggled with sodden clay and a cheap food policy: There was no mains water and in this foggy, marshy place, no mains drainage.

In 1966 those who lived here came together to facilitate proper development through a private company. With the power of the Land Commission to pull together so fractured a title as the ownership of Cheswick had become, Cheswick Green was created amongst the water meadows and the ancient willow trees. The largest house then sold for £8,750! Land by the Blythe is now precious.

Today we are a village. We have a school, in the village and up at the church. We have a family church in the village, a parish church on the hill. We have a grocer, a hairdresser, a post office. How many older villages can say as much? We have regular bus services to Solihull and even Birmingham. We have Girl Guides, Brownies, Boys Brigade, Boy Scouts, Cubs and a WI. Come and see us on Bonfire Night, down by the river, where it all started, there on the village green we have a lovely bonfire, proper bonfire food and splendid fireworks, courtesy of Cheswick Green, Village of the Seventies.

Coseley 🌿

Coseley is situated about three miles north of Dudley and, like other villages surrounding this expanding centre, has been taken into the Metropolitan Borough. It, like Brierley Hill, was largely created by the Industrial Revolution, rather than evolving from an ancient parish.

A possible derivation of the name Coseley is from 'Colresleye', 'The charcoal burners' wood'. This is mentioned in Lady Wulfruna's Charter in AD 994.

A 16th century writer describes her Well of Healing as:-

'Ladie Wulfruna's Sprynge wher shee usyd to come and washe ... it hathe curyd manie as it were myraculouslie healynge ye lamie, ye weake, ye infirme, as manie ther be can testyfie.'

The region developed rapidly as a centre for coal mining. The parish church, Christ Church, was built in 1830 by Thomas Lee. An Ebenezer Baptist chapel was also built in Birmingham New Road in 1856. A windmill in Oak Street, minus its sails, was long ago converted to a house.

Coundon 🐝

The name Coundon, although united with that of its neighbour Keresley in the designation of the parish church, is of much more ancient origin, going back perhaps to Old Celtic, 'cound', a river. A variety of spellings appear down the centuries – Cuenetford, Condelme, Cunedealme and Coundolme. Most authorities agree in connecting it with water, a ford or the confluence of rivers. The Wash Brook runs south through the area to join the river Sherbourne. Other streams mentioned in medieval documents were the Frith Brook and the Foxwell.

The hamlet appears in the Domesday Book, where it has a separate entry in spite of its lack of size. It was at that time an outlying estate of Coventry Priory. It is possible that Coundon was an estate, one of several, given to the priory by Leofric and Godiva after they had founded the great Benedictine church.

During the ensuing centuries various families were land-owners here. Their names, or the names of their holdings, still appear in today's names: for example, Bohun, later given as Boun, Bown and Brown (Brownshill Green Road); the North Field (Northfield Road); Holifast Waste (Hollyfast Road) and Jeffreys Field (The Jeffries).

The old parish of Coundon stretched south-east toward the city of Coventry but was not included in the County as formed in 1451. It became a civil parish in 1881 and in 1928 Coventry reached out and claimed 36 acres of it. Since then, the city has steadily marched north-west so that much of the area is now solidly built-up. Its farther reaches, however, remain pleasantly rural and agricultural, lying northward to the hamlet of Browns-hill Green and to Corley and westward to Allesley and the contro-versial Coundon Wedge.

In Coundon in early times, as in Keresley, hard-won clearings in the forest slowly became fields and farms with stretches of wood-land and common. Agriculture and stock-rearing remained the main source of employment until the Coventry factories began to offer industrial work.

Some of the early stock farms became large and profitable and rich medieval merchants leased or purchased land. Parcels of land were bequeathed to Coventry charities and others were gifted to the priory.

The population rose between 1086 and the 1300s and fell again in the 14th to the 16th centuries. Cottages recorded as being built in the 14th century were described as derelict in the early 15th and many of the old family names disappeared in the same period. It is tempting to ascribe these changes to the terrible devastation of the Black Death.

The wooded parts of Coundon provided work in the following centuries when faggots were made and carted to other districts. Brick-making and the quarrying of stone are suggested in old field-names such as Brick-kiln Close and Quarry Close. In the Second World War a 'shadow factory' to produce aircraft was built on the Coundon-Allesley boundary. It is now the Jaguar car factory.

During the 19th century, some of Coventry's wealthy industrial-ists bought land and built impressive houses in and around the ancient hamlet of Coundon Green, thus following in the footsteps of several medieval merchants and drapers. Alveston Cottage is the only surviving house of the older exodus from the city.

Humfrey Burton obtained the lease of the Jeffreysfield holding in 1647 and bought it in 1667. He was Town Clerk of Coventry, a meticulous man who took a great interest in the history of his city. He compiled a manuscript book known as 'Humfrey Burton's Book', into which he copied many invaluable records and docu-ments, including the very important Tripartite Indenture of 1355, settling finally the long dispute between 'The Prior's Half' and 'The Earl's Half' which had divided the city. The original document was lost. He had a hand in the Governing Charter granted by King James I in 1621, according to which the affairs of Coventry were managed well into the 19th century.

Towards the end of the 19th century, two well-known names appeared among those of Coundon residents. George Singer of Singer Cars built a fine house, Coundon Court, which became a focal point for the social life of the place. Later it passed into the hands of Captain Miller and is now a comprehensive school. The Rotherham family of watch-making fame lived in The Grange. The house is now a children's home.

Stand in the south-east half of Coundon, among the terraced houses, the pubs, shops and schools with the traffic roaring past, and its medieval people and their way of life seem a thousand years away. The building-up and levelling-out of urban development have blurred the profile of the old parish. But make a journey of only minutes to the north-west and the scene changes. In Scots Lane, with its houses and bungalows of very recent construction, look at the great oaks – or the sadly-mutilated remains of those not yet felled – and see how they marked out the ancient trackway that this once was when it formed part of Coundon's southeast boundary. A little farther on, Coundon Park is skirted by Waste Lane, once a footpath to the waste or common. Here, more of the land lies open, with school playing fields and a public park (once the grounds of Coundon Hall) and to the west, acres of rolling farmland. Here it is easy to imagine the Saxon settler laboriously hewing out his clearing from the forest; the medieval city butcher Thomas Disher coming to look over his fat-stock grazing; perhaps even the great Prior himself on horseback, inspecting his latest acquisition, the land given to the priory by William Stevens to purchase absolution for the murder of his neighbour, Walter Lewin; or the Victorian businessmen driving in their comfortable carriages to the church of St Thomas on Tamworth Road.

Darlaston 🦢

Although not mentioned in the Domesday Book, Darlaston is an ancient village, mentioned in documents concerning William de Darlaston in 1245. It is now a south-western suburb of Walsall.

There are various suggestions for the origin of the name Darlaston. It is possible that it refers to the 'Place of the Greywater'. The coal shale would, undoubtedly, have given the water its colour.

Darlaston was originally part of the parish of Sedgley. By the late 18th century trades such as gunlock maker and stirrup maker could be found here, as well as miners. Then in the 19th century Darlaston became a centre for the coal and iron industry. At the heart of the Black Country, it has played its part in the economic development of Great Britain. The Darlaston Steel & Iron Company at its peak owned 43 pudding furnaces, three blast furnaces, 63 steam engines, eight rolling mills and an internal railway system. The company was badly hit by a slump in the 1870s.

The hard lives of those who worked here demanded heroes who were larger than life, and one who fitted the bill was an innkeeper called Moses Whitehouse, nicknamed 'Rough Moey'. Born in about 1779, he must have been an awe-inspiring sight – his face pitted and scarred by smallpox and by a pit explosion, he had only one eye and one leg. His exploits, often violent, appealed to the men and women of those hard times. Though now a legend, it seems a distinct possibility that Rough Moey did indeed exist.

The George Rose Park was opened to the public in 1924, the land having been donated by Mr George Rose. The depression of the inter-war years brought unemployment to Darlaston, and it was a common sight to see men queueing in the park for the soup kitchens which were set up there to try to alleviate the worst of the distress.

Bolts, nuts, screws and rivets have all been made in the area. Other industries have included drop forgings, cycles, precast concrete, tractor parts, twines and ropes, soap and candles. Also galvanised holloware and brick making. There are large and useful varieties of clay in the district for bricks, flower pots, chimneys and tiles in large quantities.

One well known resident at the end of the last century was Mrs Henry Wood, the author of *East Lynne*. She did much to help and support the town. The setting up of a free lending library had much to do with her efforts and support.

Despite the age of the village, the parish church of St Lawrence was built only in the early 1870s. There is in fact little to remind us now of the distant past.

Dorridge 🌿

George Frederick Muntz, landowner, having given permission for the Great Western Railway to lay a track across his land, insisted upon the provision of a station from which local businessmen could travel with ease to London. He thus helped create the popular Birmingham, Oxford, Paddington route, with an express train departing from Dorridge for London at 7.45 am, returning from Paddington at 5.10 pm. Originally the approach to the station was a private road and was closed on Good Friday each year until sold to the local council in the 1960s.

Until the railway was built from London to Birmingham in 1852 there was no village of Dorridge. The area was called North Packwood and was in Packwood parish, within easy distance of Stratford Upon Avon, Warwick, Coventry and the Cotswolds and only a short train ride from Birmingham. Dorridge today is a popular residential area. Birmingham Airport is 'just down the road'. It was only after the railway was built that shops and houses came, therefore it can be considered to be a railway village.

After 1865 it was suggested that Dorridge should have its own church and in 1873 an appeal for funds was made to erect a chapel which would enable the people of Dorridge to worship in their own parish. A plot of land was given near the station by Philip Wykeham-Martin MP, a man who owned many acres in Dorridge. The church was to cost £825, but even then inflation caused the cost to be nearly £1,000 when it was completed in 1878. Within ten years it was found that the church was too small and in 1894 a churchwarden offered a sum of £500 for enlargement on condition that a similar amount was raised by December of that year. This amount was duly contributed and in 1897 a further extension was dedicated, but it was not until 1966 that Dorridge became a separate parish. Since that time the congregation has continued to grow.

Gas was made at the Knowle Gas Works, Station Road, Dorridge and supplied the needs of the village. It was put into the church in 1888. This was a private company, with local men as shareholders. It was later merged into the Solihull Gas Company. The ground is now used by Messrs Eveson's Fuel Merchants. Close by the gas works was the cattle market and slaughterhouse. Next to that was a popular hostelry known as The Vine, which was also used as a bank on market day.

Situated in Grange Road, is The Chrysanthemum Specialist Company of H. Woolman Limited. It has been a leading horticultural mail order firm for over 100 years. The company's chrysanthemums are sent all over the world, at present under the guidance of the third generation, Jack Woolman, who is President of the National Chrysanthemum Society, while the fourth generation, John G. Woolman, is President of the Midland Group of the National Chrysanthemum Society.

Edith Holden, the 'Edwardian Lady' of 'Diary' fame, had interesting connections with Dorridge. She was a great naturalist and artist, whose beautifully and accurately illustrated diary was published in the 1970s. Edith and her family were resident for ten years in a small village nearby called Darley Green. Later they moved to a house called 'Woodside' on the edge of Dorridge Wood. During this time she successfully exhibited her paintings at the Royal Birmingham Society of Artists. Edith walked or cycled in and around Dorridge gathering material for her nature diary. Many of the walks she describes can still be traversed in the lovely countryside around Dorridge.

Dorridge Park was originally a field of several acres owned by a Mr Harold Ford, whose primary aim was to build on it. Permission was refused and so in an act of great generosity in approximately 1969, he donated it to the community. It is not a park in the formal sense, but is more like a common. Some years ago the local council wanted to formalise it, but with pressure from the local people who wished to keep it as it is, the plan was dropped. There is an avenue of lovely mature trees, making it a cool shady walk on a hot day. Along this path are two seats presented by the Dorridge WI.

Dorridge has expanded a great deal since the 1960s. A growing population puts pressure on all local resources and it was felt the village was in danger of losing its identity.

In the early 1970s there was a need for a community hall for use as a focal point for local activities. The Dorridge Village Hall Association was formed with representatives from local organisations, and in 1974 they organised the first 'Dorridge Day' to be held in Dorridge Park. The first event was a tremendous undertaking but a great success, which encouraged the committee to establish the fete on an annual basis. 'Dorridge Day' is a social event enjoyed by many people. With more growth yet to come in the area the need to retain a centre for the village is strong and so 'Dorridge Day' draws on the united efforts of the community. Dorridge village hall was opened by the Mayor of Solihull in May 1976.

Dorridge is today a pleasant residental village with little local industry, with primary schools, but no secondary school. There are two small shopping precincts and cricket and tennis clubs within its boundaries. It has an ideal location on the edge of beautiful Warwickshire countryside, good access to other country towns and sights and is only half an hour from Birmingham.

Earlswood & Salter Street

Earlswood is situated in the northern part of the parish of Tanworth-in-Arden between Tanworth and Shirley, West Midlands. It was formerly part of a densely wooded waste, the name signifying part of the wood of the lords of the manor, the Earls of Warwick.

In the reign of Richard III, William Catesby had a grant from the King of 100 oaks, to be taken from the Kings' Old Park at Tanworth and Earlswood in Tanworth.

A notable feature of Earlswood is the Moathouse. This property was owned by the Misses Smythe who generously presented the old house to the nation. It is one of the oldest houses in the parish. Portions of the house date back to 1480 and the moat which still exists is much older than that. The dairy with two rooms above it is the oldest part of the house. One of the two rooms is known as the Ashbery Room, owing to the name of John Ashbery being scratched on a pane of glass in the lead latticed window. The remainder of the house dates from 1550.

Salter Street is first mentioned in Beighton Maps of Warwickshire 1722–5. At that time John Salter was living at the old moated farmhouse that later became known as Salter Street Farm, and the lane leading to his house became known as Salter Street. The farm later became the property of Mr Alfred Noakes.

After the death of John Salter his name was preserved for ever by being given to the newly created parish of Salter Street. The village church is dedicated to St Patrick, and is situated one mile north of the village of Earlswood.

St Patrick's church was built with funds which became available in an unusual manner. In 1793 the canal had been cut through this part of the parish and in 1825 the canal company made a reservoir at Earlswood for the purpose of feeding the canal. To do this they took 51 acres of Earlswood common land for which they paid £969 8s 6d to the churchwardens of Tanworth, to be held in trust. On the 9th October 1827 the churchwardens held a meeting to decide what to do with the money in their possession. Those at the meeting decided that a chapel should be built, but the trustees did not appear to be in a hurry to do this, and an old saying has it that the Powers of Darkness were against them! A piece of land was finally purchased from a Miss Heynes and the chapel was built where the present church stands, completed in 1840.

The original church of St Patrick was a simple brick building containing two galleries, one for the men and one for the women. In 1861 Thomas Burman erected the tower at a cost of £1,200, in memory of his parents. In 1899 the church was rebuilt with money donated by Miss Elizabeth Burman.

The interior of the church has been made very beautiful, largely by the generous gifts of the Misses Mynors, who in 1910 gave the stained glass east window, the holy table, reredos, the beautifully carved oak chancel screen, the clergy desks and the choir stalls, and in 1913, a new organ.

Mr Harry Bullivant was the wheelwright of Salter Street and Mr Batchelor was the blacksmith. The other blacksmith was Mr Pace, who lived in a small cottage in Umberslade Road. There was also plenty of work for labourers in the shape of thatching, hedge laying, mole catching and hay tying.

Bank Holidays were a local day out for Birmingham people, mostly conveyed out to Earlswood by horse-drawn carriages. There were, and are now, three inns – The Red Lion, the Bulls Head and the Reservoir, where they would have their meals. A Mr Parrok kept the Reservoir Hotel and by all accounts was the most amusing. Not very tall, he had a walrus moustache, wore a bowler hat, a yellow waistcoat and spats! The butchers would come out on a Monday in gigs, and races were held down on the common.

The three reservoirs in Earlswood are man-made and were built for filling the canal, which in turn was used for refilling the locomotives for the Great Western Railway. British Waterways now own the lakes.

At one time there was a brickyard at Biddles Hill, as well as a brick kiln in Lady Lane where they turned out handmade bricks, some of which were used to build the Reservoir Hotel.

In Small Lane is still Fowlers Dairy Farm, where local cheese is made, and people come from near and far to buy, although it is widely distributed.

The Blue Bell Inn in Warings Green used to be owned by a local family named Lucas, who brewed their own beer on the premises. It was a real country pub, with sides of bacon hanging in the bar, and every day the local baker would deliver home-made bread. Cottage loaves were cut into chunks and placed on the counter with cheese and pickled onions, and all this was free to have with your pint. All the barges on the canal made a stopping place there.

The first tarmac roads were surfaced in 1921. Until then they were just country lanes with grass growing up the middle of the road. Today it is very different, very built up, with no time to stand and stare, but it is nice to look back at the past.

Eastern Green 🦢

Eastern Green is only a short distance from Meriden, the centre of England. Although now joined to Coventry and only twelve miles from Birmingham, it still has its own identity, which makes what is largely a residential area a very pleasant place to live.

Historically, the area of Eastern Green had an interesting network of roads, the majority of which have disappeared as roads

Old wheelwright's cottage, Eastern Green

but have been preserved as footpaths. One of these was shown by John Ogilby in his road map of 1675, this being Sherles or Sherley's Lane which ran from Pickford Grange Farm to Back Lane. Pickford Green Lane is also an old thoroughfare, once called Workhouse Lane from the fact that Blythe House was used as the Allesley parish workhouse from 1790 to 1820.

Originally the area of Eastern Green was encompassed by nearby Allesley. In 1875 the parish church of St Andrew was consecrated, having been built with money endowed by Elizabeth Morgan. It is constructed of red bricks with Bath stone dressings in the style of the 13th century. It is worthy of note that only 56 houses stood in the parish in the year of its consecration, contrasting with today's figure of some 3,000 plus.

Eastern Green's proximity to Coventry did not mean that the city was easily reached and relative isolation meant that the community could boast its own butcher's shop, tin-smith, several laundries, a blacksmith and a wheelwright. We are told that it always had two public houses, The Old Unicorn and one which rejoiced in having the name of The Rag and Louse.

Years ago on the corner of Upper Eastern Green Lane and Pickford Green Lane stood the village blacksmith's shed. Prior to about 1920 a Mr Holmes lived at Corner Cottage, and the corner site was surrounded by various buildings and worksheds. Mr Holmes moved to a farm a few doors away but still carried on his one-man business until just before the start of the Second World War.

Often the children coming home from the nearby village school gathered around to watch the fire glowing and the sparks flying as the hand bellows were pumped and the shoes forged prior to fitting to the carthorses of the district. Mr Holmes was also the village carpenter and wheelwright. He built ladders, five-barred gates and carts. As well as these crafts he also had another occupation. He helped out as the village undertaker, constructing coffins in the required two or three days by working late into the night by the light of hurricane lamps. Many Eastern Green people will remember Holmes's sheds and the walks to post letters in the old Victorian pillar box in the smithy wall. Corner Cottage is still standing today and is a listed building subject to a preservation order, the inside walls being a fine example of wattle and daub.

In those dim and distant days the pace of life was different, the traffic slower, Eastern Green Lane was just a track used only by horse-drawn carts. Hockley Lane was so narrow the hedges would bend over and touch and with little traffic, football and cricket were played in the road. Respected by all, the appearance of the village constable would guarantee that 'stumps were pulled' before 'ears were cuffed' if he thought it necessary. The first local motor car was seen in 1903 and was owned by Rev Sutton. Sutton Avenue stands to his memory today.

The village school at the turn of the century used a slate and pencil, water was drawn from a pump and placed in a bucket for the children to drink using a communal mug chained to the wall. The pump can still be seen in the garden of School House today.

The original village hall was housed in a disused army hut which was purchased for £75 during Mr Despard's time as vicar (from

60

1913 to 1937). During the Second World War it was requisitioned by the RAF and housed barrage balloon personnel. Following the war the need was recognised for a larger village hall in view of the fact that a large portion of Eastcote Farm had been sold for housing development and plans for enlarging Eastern Green were already in hand. Nowhere within a radius of five miles was there a hall large enough to serve the needs of the expanding population. A portion of land was purchased by the late Mr W. B. Neal at a public auction in 1945, who then relinquished all claims on repayment of the cost. Money for building the parish hall was raised in many ways. Weekly door to door collections were organised, as well as raffles and a field day. A tea room in the old parish room was installed to raise funds and preceded the opening of a licensed bar, which became the forerunner of the affiliated social club standing in Church Lane today. The new village hall was opened in 1958 and has since proved to be a valuable asset to the community, accommodating so many activities and organisations.

Recent development has altered the face of Eastern Green. Houses have sprung up and the community has changed from earning its living in agriculture to industry and commerce, but in spite of this it has kept its village characteristics – within easy reach of Coventry city centre and on the doorstep of the beautiful Warwickshire countryside.

Edgbaston ✤

Edgbaston is situated barely one mile from the centre of Birmingham. It has a remarkable history. In the Domesday Book of 1086 it was identified as 'Celboldestone' and was valued at 30 shillings. From the 13th century there were references to Edgbaston church (St Bartholomew's, known locally as Edgbaston Old Church) and, somewhat later, to a manor house (since 1936, Edgbaston Golf Club). The lordship passed from the de Egbaldeston family to the Middlemores sometime in the 15th century. Until well into the 18th century Edgbaston remained a parish of scattered farms, labourer's cottages and small watermills, with no identifiable village nucleus.

A key event in its history occurred in 1717 when the lordship, which comprised some two-thirds of the parish of 3,000 acres, was sold to Sir Richard Gough, a successful East India merchant, for £20,400. He rebuilt the church and the hall, both of which had been ruined during the Civil War, added a deer park and settled down to the life of a rural squire. The estate has been continuously in the hands of the same family ever since, although they are better known as the Calthorpes. This name derived from a marriage alliance which brought the family extensive estates in East Anglia and Hampshire and, when Sir Richard's grandson was raised to the peerage in 1796, he took the title of Calthorpe. It was to be the estate in Edgbaston, however, which was to be the family's golden goose.

By the late 18th century Edgbaston's rural tranquillity was increasingly threatened by the looming proximity of the fastest growing industrial town in Britain. Without the unity of control provided by the existence of a dominant ground landlord, Edgbaston would surely have succumbed, like other areas, to a tide of workshops and back-to-back houses. It was preserved from this fate by the third lord (1807–1851) and his agent, John Harris. Between them they laid the foundations of a high-class residential area which was designed to attract the industrial and commercial elite of Birmingham. Streets and sewers were laid out and blocks of land were leased for building plots. Building plans were carefully vetted and leases strictly drawn to prevent any form of commercial or industrial activity. The estate gradually filled with elegant and spacious residences, though around the fringes there were both lower middle class and working class developments.

By the 1880s the estate had reached its apogee and was widely admired as one of the finest residential suburbs in Britain, the jewel in Birmingham's smokey crown. Its population included a high proportion of Birmingham's best known families – the Chamberlains, Kenricks, Martineaus, Beales etc. It has rightly been described as 'the Council House at home'.

To add to its attractiveness the Calthorpes endowed a host of institutions – the Botanical Gardens, the Deaf and Dumb and the Blind Institutes, prestigious schools and several additional churches. The first-ever game of lawn tennis was played on a private lawn in Edgbaston, while Edgbaston Archery and Lawn

Tennis Society, tucked away behind the Botanical Gardens, is one of the oldest lawn tennis clubs in the world. In 1885 Edgbaston also became the home of Warwickshire County Cricket Club. Early in the new century, the Calthorpes donated 45 acres of land to endow the University of Birmingham, its impressive central buildings complete by 1909.

By 1914 Edgbaston had passed its peak. Instead of being the 'West End' of Birmingham, it had by then become an inner suburb with other, newer suburbs developing beyond its boundaries. In the 18th century it had survived the challenge of the canal, in the 19th century that of the railways. In the 20th century it faced the onslaught of tramways, buses and the tide of commuter traffic. Many of its richer families migrated to more distant parts. Yet in many respects it changed remarkably little until the 1950s. Then, however, it was forced to adapt to commercial pressures. The area around Five Ways, in the north-east corner of the estate, and along the Hagley Road became an area of office blocks and hotels, identified as Birmingham's Croydon. Many of the elegant 19th century houses in adjoining streets ceased to be residential, and instead housed architects, solicitors, accountants and consultants. Many of the larger houses in the centre of the estate were demolished to make way for estates of modern middle-class housing.

Much evidence of Edgbaston's elegant past, however, remains: excellent streets like Wellington Road and Frederick Road, many fine buildings, beautiful trees, and important institutions. For all the changes, Edgbaston remains Birmingham's premier suburb.

Forshaw Heath 🦊

Forshaw Heath, just one and a half miles long and roughly one and a quarter miles wide, has had a very tranquil history.

It was in existence in the 9th century, when it was known as Foxshawe, the place of foxes. Foxshawe came within the influence of Solihull and the owner of a large moated house paid one penny a year as a tithe. The remains of the moat are still to be seen – a muddy waterway in the middle of a field.

Solihull's interest declined and Forshaw Heath, as it was now called, became part of the domain of Stratford-on-Avon and remains so to this day. There has been little turbulence known in the district.

The other large house is Forshaw Park Farm, a very beautiful, well restored place which has been occupied since 1624. The house together with its huge barn are now listed buildings. In the 1930s it was occupied by a very eccentric character named Harry Seager. He lived and worked nights and slept in the day in a dreadful old chair. He never went upstairs. He wandered about the district on his old horse, *Dolly*, but he was a wonderful naturalist.

Harry had a theory that at one time the sea reached Forshaw and the only hill, 'Biddles Hill', is really a cliff. He had a huge collection of sea shells, which he had gathered locally to reinforce his ideas. Shells can still be found in the woods.

These woods are part of the Forest of Arden. They are very lovely in the spring with bluebells, lilies of the valley, marsh marigolds and foxgloves. There is also a very fine sweet chestnut tree. The Turkey oak also here, is said to be hundreds of years old.

This is our quiet Forshaw Heath, at least it still is, but 'times are a changing', now that we have the M42 on our doorstep.

Four Oaks 🦋

On the A5127, two miles north of Sutton Coldfield, lies Four Oaks, a small bustling spot which was originally a quiet rural area consisting of cornfields, small cottages, farms, one pub and a post office.

On the west side of the main Lichfield Road is Four Oaks estate, which originally stretched from Bracebridge Road to Hartopp Road and was known as Four Oaks Park. It contained Four Oaks Hall, built at the end of the 17th century and the home of Simon Luttrell. In 1792 it became the home of Edmund Hartopp and later Sir John Hartopp. Hence Luttrell Road and Hartopp Road. The Park also contained a dower house, cottages, a vinery and lodges, and the original four oak trees stood in the grounds of one of the lodges in Hartopp Road. The hall has long since been demolished. Four Oaks at one time had a racecourse, but this too is long gone.

Four Oaks Park is now a private housing estate and contains prestigious houses with large grounds, an abundance of trees and is a wonderful rhododendron area. It backs onto Sutton Park and some houses are lucky enough to have their own entrances into the park.

Also on the west side lies Butlers Lane railway station. One villager recalls Sunday school outings from Erdington station to Butlers Lane, where all the children alighted from the train in frolicsome mood ready to run riot in the open fields and let off steam.

To the east side of the main road stands Moor Hall, now an hotel and golf course, and within its grounds stands the house which was the birthplace of Bishop Vesey, who was a great benefactor of Sutton Coldfield, and after whom the local grammar school was named. The majority of its estate grounds were sold off and made into a housing estate consisting of bungalows, detached and semi-detached houses.

At the beginning of the 20th century there were seven farms in Four Oaks. The local inhabitants would go to the farms for dairy produce. Groceries would be delivered. Wealthy people with carriers fetched their own coal from the Black Country. Children were taught to curtsy to the vicar and School Attendance Officer and to learn the scriptures off by heart. Roads were not metalled and there were no street lamps. There are still a few farms left and now, as in many other areas, produce can be bought from the Farm Shop. Two of the farms now stable horses for their owners.

There are three churches; St James, built at the beginning of the 19th century, All Saints, built in 1908 and Four Oaks Methodist church, all of which are well attended by their parishioners. In the 1980s a new Catholic church was built on the main Lichfield Road.

Not too many years ago on the main road stood Primroses Cottages. They were charming but, alas, these have disappeared and in their place stand supermarkets and other shops.

In the 1930s the Nottingham to Birmingham Walk sponsored by the *Sunday Mercury* would take place and competitors would pass through Mere Green, pausing at The Forge Cafe, for brief refreshment.

Since the 1960s the face of Mere Green and Four Oaks has

changed dramatically. The shopping area has vastly increased. There are now five banks, at least four building societies and five estate agents, three supermarkets, plus many other shops, all of which thrive. The original pub, now called The Barleys, still stands at the corner of Belwell Lane and Lichfield Road.

There is a little industry as Lucas Electrical and Probus Kitchenware have small factories in Mere Green Road, but this is likely to change.

Further down the main road is Four Oaks railway station, which is well patronised by commuters to Birmingham. This station was built originally because of an agricultural fair which was held here. Once again the old railway cottages have been demolished and in their place stands the station car park, which is always full.

Quite a few schools have shot up, due to the housing expansion, whereas in the past there were two – a private preparatory school and the local village school (now a restaurant).

Great Barr 🦃

There is no better place to see the meeting of ancient and modern than in the one-time village of Great Barr. It is dominated by the hill called Barr Beacon, seen for miles around the Midlands and by the 20th century motorway interchange for north, south and west. The speeding motorway traffic passes through, unaware of a village rich in history but now part of an urban conurbation.

In the Domesday Book, Great Barr was mentioned along with Aldridge. William the Conqueror gave the land to William Fitz-Ansculf of Dudley.

By 1378 the population consisted of 74 people. A chapel of ease had been built at Great Barr on the site of the present-day St Margaret's church. By 1677 the chapel was rebuilt into a more solid structure with a tower and a steeple and by this time the influence of the Scott family was prominent.

They were the most important family from Tudor times until the 20th century. At this time they resided in the Old Hall at Great Barr. Farmland consisted of open fields with strips until the 16th century when the fields were enclosed. There is a record of Great

Barr figuring in a case at the Court of the Star Chamber over a land dispute.

The Scott family reached the sphere of greatest influence in the 18th century. They had been granted a baronetcy and Sir Joseph Scott built a new Great Barr Hall, a splendid example of Gothic revival architecture similar to that built by Sir Horace Walpole at Strawberry Hill at Twickenham. Alas, Great Barr Hall has now been allowed to lapse into a shocking state of disrepair and seems doomed to perish.

Sir Joseph was a colourful character involved in many wheelings and dealings. He squandered three fortunes and was lucky in that Thomas Hoo, lord of the manor of Great Barr, died intestate and named Sir Joseph's wife as an heiress. But even this had to survive a court appeal. In his time the famous Lunar Society often met at the Hall with members like Boulton, Watt and Priestly.

Sir Joseph's son, the second baronet, also hit the headlines. He married twice, the second time to a Lydia Robinson reputed to be the unrequited love of Bramwell Bronte, the unfortunate ailing brother of the Bronte sisters. Mrs Gaskell in a biography of Charlotte Bronte went as far as to mention that Lydia was Bramwell's 'paramour'. The outraged Scott family threatened libel and Mrs Gaskell was forced to apologise in a letter to *The Times*.

The third baronet, Sir Francis Edward Scott, richly endowed the building of a new St Margaret's church in 1862 and it is now recognised as one of the most beautiful churches in the district. The widow of Sir Edward contrived to dominate the district until the early 20th century. After her death the Hall was sold to the West Bromwich & Walsall Board of Governors and later became a hospital for the mentally handicapped.

An infamous character who lived in Great Barr was the noted forger, William Booth, who was the only man to be hanged twice. He is remembered by a road, Booth's Farm Road, called after the farm he inhabited.

By 1921 the population of Great Barr was 2,232 and it was a peaceful rural community comprising farmland and several large houses. Roads now thick with traffic were country lanes where the movement of cattle caused the only blockage. The Scott Arms public house was a landmark and local gathering place. Here the Coroner held his court and it housed the local mortuary.

Many villagers can recall attending the village Church of England school at St Margaret's which dates back to the 19th century. One of the large estates held the Red House, which became a convalescent home in the First World War and later a public park.

As a memorial to the soldiers who fell in the First World War the Great Barr Memorial Hall was built in 1926 to be used as a social gathering place for the people of Great Barr.

With increasing industrialisation and the population explosion, Great Barr changed in the 1930s to become an area of housing estates, the farms and gracious houses giving way to red brick developments. Gas and electricity were established in the 1920s and schools, churches and shops were built. It is a thriving, busy place today but the community spirit is fostered in institutions, churches and schools.

Barr Beacon, the dominating landmark, has seen many changes since the entry in Domesday and will see many more. The beacon may have been used to warn of the Armada in 1588. It was certainly used in Napoleonic times and to celebrate Queen Victoria's Jubilees. As recently as 1988 it was lit to celebrate the 400th anniversary of the Armada.

Beneath it run the motorways and the enormous electric pylons carrying power across the country, 'like whips of anger, with lightning danger, there runs the quick perspective of the future' (William Spender).

Hall Green 🐚

The settlement of Hall Green, now a suburb of Birmingham, has a very long history. In AD 972 a Saxon settlement known as Gyrdeleahe (later to become Yardley) was granted to the Abbey of Pershore. Included in Gyrdeleahe was the area we now know as Hall Green.

In 1327 Agret Haw(e) is recorded as paying 6½d in the Subsidy Roll of Yardley parish, and his Hall stood on land adjacent to the present School Road and Fox Hollies Road. The Hall and district became known as Haw(e) Green.

Another occupant of Hawe Green Hall was Job Marston. He died in 1701, and he must have been a wealthy man because he bequeathed land across the green from Hawe Green Hall, plus £1,000, for a chapel of ease to be built. He also left £1,200 for maintenance and a priest. The chapel was consecrated in 1704 having been designed by Sir William Wilson, the son of a Leicestershire baker, and a protégé of Sir Christopher Wren. In 1907 the chapel of ease became the parish church, and in 1954 it became the Church of Ascension.

Hawe Green Hall was sold and later demolished, and replaced by almshouses in 1936. Lewis E. Lloyd and his wife Gertrude who had lived at Hawe Green Hall were shocked when they saw the Hall demolished. They were under the impression that it was to continue as a family residence.

Hawe Green Hall was not the only notable residence. There was also the Hollies, occupied by the Fox family. The Hollies was an

Sarehole Mill, now a museum, at Hall Green

imposing building approached through an avenue of trees. The trees still stand along Greenwood Avenue, but all that remains of the impressive Hall is a gate pillar.

Street and road names can be traced back to family names or to occupations, for example School Road and Fox Hollies Road. Studland Road was so called because horses were at one time bred on land near Hawe Green Hall and the locals called it Stud Land.

Hall Green has a few public houses. The Bull's Head is an old hostelry, with the now busy Birmingham to Stratford-on-Avon road passing by. Further along the road is the Robin Hood public house, but the history of that building does not go so far back in time. It was a private residence until it was put up for sale in 1876. However, a small inn with the same name earlier stood on land close by. Close to the inn six ways converged and the area was not known then as Robin Hood Island, but it was Six Ways. Although there are still six ways from Robin Hood Island it is a very different design, and car drivers have to be aware of the many sets of traffic lights at the island.

Old maps show that there were at least six water-mills in the area, but the only remaining water-mill is Sarehole Mill which stands on the boundary between Hall Green and Moseley, by the side of the river Cole. Sarehole Mill was opened as a branch museum on 12th July, 1969. The building in its present form dates from the 18th century but there has probably been a mill at Sarehole since the Middle Ages. The mill was bequeathed to the City of Birmingham in 1946, but through lack of funds the building was allowed to deteriorate. Local residents asked for an appeal fund to be launched, and now the mill is visited by many people and used in television plays and documentaries.

Other amenities in the area include bowling greens, and also a greyhound stadium. There are tennis courts and various other sporting activities, but the horse racing course has gone.

From Leommansweg in the 10th century to Stratford Road in the 20th century. From people trudging along gutted ways to cars speeding along the smooth tarmac. Times have changed. In 1939 Hall Green had its major shopping area along Stratford Road. There were two cinemas, Rialto and Robin Hood, a police station, post office, and good public transport. Now the cinemas have been replaced by supermarkets. Shops have changed hands. Shop frontages have changed appearances. Petrol stations have come and gone, and come again. There are no longer traces of tram-lines along Stratford Road, but there are buses, and an almost continuous stream of daylight traffic, and for those who wish to travel by train there are local trains.

Hall Green has several good examples of 19th century buildings, such as the school on Stratford Road – a solid red brick building with many different styles of windows, and topped by a bell tower. Opposite to the school there is another building of architectural interest – the Society of Friends meeting house. Look at the unusual chimneys. Now planners are pressing ahead to preserve 20th century houses. They are hoping to preserve two streets of 1930s semis as part of Birmingham's architectural heritage. City Councillors are being recommended to earmark part of School Road and Miall Road for designation as a conservation area. They would be the first relatively modern homes in the city, and among the first in the country, to be given such status.

In addition to Birmingham being known as an industrial city it has been the father to many famous people and Hall Green lays claim to its quota. Tony Hancock, the comedian and actor was born at 41, Southam Road. The author J. R. R. Tolkien who lived in Wake Green Road, gleaned inspiration for his book *Lord of the Rings* from the area.

It is said that only people who live just a stone's throw away from the Church of Ascension can claim to be residents of Hall Green, but many people who live within the boundary are proud to say they live in Hall Green, especially those whose memories can go back more than a couple of decades.

Hampton-in-Arden

The parish church, begun in 1130 on the site of an old Saxon church, celebrated its 850th anniversary in 1980. A number of Norman features still remain, including a doorway and an old south wall. Many alterations have taken place over the centuries but the stone benches along the wall still remain from an age when worshippers stood and 'the weakest went to the wall'. There is also a Heart Tomb in the chancel, which probably once contained the heart of a Knight Templar.

The tower was once topped by a spire – this fell during a great

Packhorse bridge, Hampton in Arden

storm in 1643. Hampton had at one time been mother church to the outlying districts of Knowle, Nuthurst, Temple Balsall, Chadwick and Baddesley Clinton. In the late 14th century, Knowle parishioners got tired of the long walk of crossing the river to Hampton and built their own church and from then on refused to assist with expenses and dues to Hampton church. They therefore refused to help when Hampton was required, by the Court at Warwick, to rebuild the spire. By Easter 1654 Hampton too had refused to pay for rebuilding and so Hampton has no steeple!

Inside the church, many memorials give an idea of the people who have lived at Hampton during the ages and include names still well known in the village. The processional cross, given in 1968 in memory of Norman Pegg, a long serving churchwarden, has a small mouse carved on its staff, the signature of the Thompson family, woodcarvers of Yorkshire.

Hampton is lucky in that its church registers date back to 1599 and make interesting and sometimes amusing reading. The east window was given by Sir Frederick Peel in memory of his first wife and the chancel screen was given in his memory by his second wife. Peel's father, Sir Robert Peel (well known for his work in instituting a modern police force) built the present manor for his son. Sir Frederick, an MP, was also much involved with the railway age and the growth of Hampton can be seen in that, from a farming community in the 19th century (several of the old farms still remain – albeit with small acreages), new houses, both small and large appeared around the railway. Houses in the High Street were built as part of the manor estate. At this time Sir Frederick and Lady Peel were generous contributors to the church and village and the fact that the manor grounds and village have so many beautiful old trees is due to his love and care of trees, many of which he planted.

Another great benefactor is surprisingly not represented in the church, being buried in St Martin's church in Birmingham. George Fentham was baptised at Hampton in 1630 and his sister married the son of the vicar, her son becoming the first known village schoolmaster. Nothing is known of George's early life until he is mentioned in documents as a Birmingham businessman giving money and help to schools and other charitable organisations.

In 1690 he made a will setting up various charities, including one for Hampton-in-Arden. It was very complicated but principally was to set up a 'School for male children of the Inhabitants of the Parish' and for the relief of the poor. This was to be done from rent etc from his properties and at that time was worth £30. It is now worth somewhat more and has provided much for the village, not only the school but the Fentham Hall and Club and Fentham Green Bungalows, and gives help in many ways as need arises. The first school, built in 1782, still stands in Fentham Road.

Since the population of the village is only about 1,800, it is surprising how many sports and other activities are available. Music and drama organisations have, through the years, waxed and waned but, at present, both are flourishing.

In 1251 Sir Hugh Arden obtained a grant to hold a weekly market and this continued until the 1960s when the old market was pulled down to make way for flats.

A local landmark, known as the 'Packhorse Bridge' and once erroneously called the 'Roman Bridge' dates from the 1500s and was part of the route used to transport salt from Droitwich to Coventry. This and other features of the village are jealously guarded by the Hampton Society, which concerns itself with attempting to protect the local environment from industrial and similar encroachments. It is thanks to them and the local Parish Council that Hampton can still be called a 'village'.

Hamstead 🖋

Hamstead Hall was the manor house of Handsworth and for nearly 400 years its history was closely linked with the Wyrley family, keepers of the Royal Chase at Cannock. The earliest reference to the family was in 1228 when William de Wyrley was the rector of Handsworth. In 1290 Guy de Wyrley, sometimes called Guy de Hamstead, lived on Hamstead Hill. Hamstead Hall was built around 1450 and was the manor house for about 250 years. The house was the centre of a substantial estate with large gardens and considerable parkland. They had their own mill, which was also used to pump water to the house from the river Tame. There were only four cottages, probably for shepherds and keepers, so it would appear that there was no village of Hamstead at that time.

A manuscript now preserved in the Herald's College on 'Inscriptions from monuments and painted windows in old Churches' was written by William Wyrley in 1604.

In 1680 Sir John Wyrley became lord of the manor of Handsworth and Hamstead and sometime before 1690 the old Hall was destroyed by fire. In 1690 Sir John commenced the rebuilding of the Hall on a site further from the river and it was further enlarged in 1735. It was said to be 'handsome and commodious with extensive grounds stretching down to the river Tame'.

Shaw's *History of Staffordshire* shows that the Wyrleys were in possession of Handsworth, Barrs, Witton, Little Aston, Hillchoe in Sutton, the manor of Tipton and a manor in Leicestershire. Their name lives on in road and place names in these areas but unfortunately not on the Hamstead Hall estate.

Following the land closures in Handsworth in 1793, George Wyrley-Birch sold the manor house and much of the estate to the Earl of Dartmouth of Sandwell Hall in 1819 and so ended the long association of the Wyrley family with Hamstead Hall.

The Hall was never again owner-occupied. At first it was used as the dower house to Sandwell Hall, followed by short leases. John Moillet, a banker from Geneva lived there in 1841, and William Bagnall, coal and ironmaster in 1861. From 1886 to 1890 the Hall was leased to George Kynoch, the Witton industrialist. He spent a great deal of money decorating and furnishing the Hall and this, together with business difficulties and the expense of a parliamentary election, ruined him. The contents of the Hall were auctioned and in addition to the furniture and china from six bedrooms and six reception rooms, there were 180 pictures, a library of 2,000 volumes, a cellar of 400 dozen choice wines, three carriages and two dog-carts.

Another tenant was Mr Kirkham, a herbalist of Smallbrook Street, who opened the grounds as an 'Entertainment Garden'. Besides boating and fishing there were clowns, a glee party, gymnasts, a huge whale (which had been carried on railway lorries placed end to end) and a lady 'with a head of glorious hair which she plaited and attached to a miniature lorry which she trailed after her as she walked'.

In Nightingale's *Beauties of England & Wales*, Hamstead grounds were described thus, 'the grounds of Hamstead winding along the river Tame are pleasing and romantic, being covered with a profusion of stately trees', but by 1854 the Tame was polluted with drainage from the Black Country and this was written:-

'The Tame was foul as it could be with
sewage black as dye
It ran with garbage in the wet and
stank when it was dry.
No fishes lay beneath its bank,
there were no fish to lie.'

In 1875 the tiny village of Hamstead on the other side of the river began to grow, with the arrival of miners and their families.

As the colliery grew in importance, so Hamstead Hall began to lose stature. The children's annual outing from Hamstead school was to the grounds of Hamstead Hall.

During the First World War the Hall was used as a hostel in connection with the war effort and it was finally demolished in 1936 when the whole area was developed for housing. Part of the old grounds along the river bank has survived as woodland and the remains of the ice-house and garden wall can still be seen.

During the excavations for the building of the new estate, a very substantial foundation was revealed on the site of the original Hall. The structure resting on this was likely to have been timber framing filled in with brickwork or wattle and daub.

The area is now a pleasant post-war development, sometimes known as the Grestone Estate (after the builders – Greaves and Johnstone), but with the name of Hamstead Hall living on in road names, the name of the secondary school and of course the WI.

The grounds were not all built on. Handsworth Golf Course and the school playing fields look over the river, which happily is running clear again, towards the Sandwell RSPB reserve. Walking along here, it is just possible to visualise what a beautiful place Hamstead Hall and its grounds must have been.

Harborne 🦋

Harborne is now a residential suburb of Birmingham, lying approximately three miles from the city centre on the South Westside, within easy reach of the motorways. At the time of the census in 1981 it covered 543 hectares with 22,143 inhabitants.

There is a great diversity of housing, including council flats, council houses, many of which are now owner-occupied, semi-detached and detached houses built since the 1930s, and some much older and bigger properties. There are new complexes for the elderly and two traditional old people's homes, St Joseph's run by the Little Sisters of the Poor, and the Grove belonging to the City of Birmingham.

There is also a thriving mixture of businesses, commerce, restaurants and excellent shopping in 'the village', still called by this name. There are churches of all denominations, infant, junior and comprehensive schools and adult education centres, one of which is at the Clock Tower in the High Street. This was originally a junior school, first opened in 1881, and now provides an interesting centre for many activities.

The oldest church in the parish is St Peter's, dating back to 1217. St John's church, also in the High Street, is a modern church with excellent facilities which replaced the original in St John's Road, destroyed by enemy action during the Second World War in 1945.

Recreational activities available in Harborne include tennis, swimming, two golf courses, a cricket club, and a hockey club formed in 1903. The latter has one of the premier teams in the country and is in the first division of the National League, its members coming from all parts of the country. There are two parks and many public houses, several of which are very old.

The Romans had a camp at Metchley within the boundary and Harborne was mentioned in the Domesday Book as Horeborne – literally meaning 'muddy brook'. The Bournbrook, a small stream still running, used to form the boundary between Staffordshire and Worcestershire. The Chad brook also runs through Harborne and this gave its name to the Chad Valley Toy Factory, regrettably now no more.

Until the late 18th century, Harborne was mostly rural. Then the High Street began to be developed towards Harborne Heath, now the site of the Green Man public house. There was a small community of nail-makers in Cammomile Green in Tennal Road, and a flourishing trade in gooseberry growing during the appropriate season.

A universal industry can be remembered in the jingle –

> 'Hungry Harborne proud and poor,
> A washerwoman at every door'.

This is attributed to the local women who lived in the Moorpool estate. They did the washing in the soft water of the Moor Pool, and this was collected on a regular basis from the big houses in adjoining Edgbaston.

The estate was founded in 1907 by John Sutton Nettlefold, and represented an early experiment in town planning, built with only nine houses to the acre at a time when 40 houses per acre were permitted. It was to provide, in an attractive setting, well built houses to let at reasonable rents. Tenants were also able to buy shares in the company so that eventually they would own and manage the estate on a co-operative basis. This is still so today, although many of the houses are privately owned. It is unique and the only small company of its kind that remains independent. The estate, which is a conservation area, still centres around the Moor Pool, which attracts wild life and Canada Geese are regular visitors. The green, where once stood a maypole, now has all-weather tennis courts. There is a bowling green and the community hall is used for many activities.

The railway just adjacent to the Moorpool estate ran into New Street station, Birmingham and was opened in 1874. The service became affectionately known as 'The Harborne Express or Flier', a misnomer, as the journey took 22 minutes going into the city and 18 minutes coming out. Passengers could even pick flowers on the way as the train stopped frequently! The line is now closed and used as a public walkway.

Many of the existing roads are named after people and houses, for example, Carless Avenue takes its name from the Carless family who lived at the Ravenhurst. Eminent men who lived in Harborne were Thomas Attwood the radical Member of Parliament, at the Grove (now just the park with no house), David Cox, the artist in Greenfield Road, and W. H. Auden, the poet, in Lordswood Road and in Court Oak Road.

In estate agent's terminology, Harborne is a 'desirable area' in which to live. This is due to the work done by the Harborne Society to maintain the old style traditions and as a watchdog for future developments, and the genuine care and interest of the residents.

Hockley Heath 🦚

Together with the hamlets of Illshaw Heath, Umberslade and Nuthurst, Hockley Heath was once known as Hnuthyrste, meaning Nut Wood, and given to the Bishop of Worcester by King Offa of Mercia. It is still ecclesiastically known as Nuthurst cum Hockley Heath. Parts of the village were left behind in Warwickshire after boundary changes in 1974.

It owes its importance to the highway running through the village, where traffic thunders along relentlessly. A far cry from the muddy track in Roman times through the woodland of Arden and over the Heath, or the turnpike road when the village was a staging post on the old mail coach road from London to Birmingham. With up to four coaches a day, places were needed where meals could be obtained, passengers refreshed and horses changed and fed. Such a coaching house was Hockley House, now unfortunately demolished to make way for modern houses. At the nearby Nags Head inn, post horses were kept.

The coming of the railways drove the horse-drawn coaches off the roads. Hockley Heath, not served directly by the railway network, became comparatively isolated except for local carriers plying between Birmingham, Warwick and Stratford upon Avon, until 1816 when the Birmingham to Stratford upon Avon Canal was opened. A wharf was built which brought much trade and served a wide area of the countryside, unloading such commodities as coal, stone, lime, bricks, salt and timber. It was known as Hockley Port, with its old salt warehouse by the Wharf Inn. The Cheshires and Gameson families were local wharfingers. The waterway was extensively used until railways again took over in 1850. After years of dereliction it is pleasure boats that now ply their way through the village.

Hockley Heath had its share of 'big' houses, with a manor at ancient Nuthurst. Still standing, but now an hotel, is Aylesbury House, originally the home of the Aylesbury family and Umberslade Hall, a large stone structure set in its own parkland. It was erected on the site of a moated manor house in the latter end of the 17th century by a member of the Archer family, a descendant of Robertus Sagittarius or Robert the Archer who came over with

William the Conqueror. Thomas Archer was created Baron Archer of Umberslade in 1747 and it is said it was he who had the obelisk erected to commemorate the honour. He was a well known architect and responsible for the design and building of Birmingham cathedral.

The next owner of the Hall was Mr E. Bolton King, an MP for Birmingham. Then followed four generations of the Muntz family, industrialists and landowners and, with Mr Bolton King, great benefactors to the village. During the Second World War, the Hall was occupied by troops, including Belgian and Czech contingents. In recent years it has been converted into private apartments.

It seems the inhabitants of Hockley Heath were a heathen and uneducated lot up to 1837, with neither church nor school. To remedy this state of affairs Mr E. Bolton King gave land for the building of a chapel, now used as a builder's workshop in Orchard Road, previously known as Chapel Lane. At the same time he gave land to build and maintain a school, which still stands at the end of School Road, now used as a storeroom. The school was closed in 1913 but reopened in 1920 to take juniors from the new overcrowded Central School. It was finally closed in 1935 and became a post office and main sorting office for mail collected and delivered over a wide area.

Because of its position on the main road from Birmingham, Hockley Heath had for more than 100 years been a central office for postal deliveries over a wide area. In 1936 letters and parcels so increased that nine men and three women were on the outdoor postal staff delivering mail by bicycle or on foot. Telegraph facilities were available as early as 1884, thanks to Mr George Frederick Muntz of Umberslade Hall. In 1845 the first postmaster was a Matthew Wood, who was also the village bootmaker and repairer. Letters arrived at Mr Wood's house by mail cart, were sorted and delivered by 7am.

Mr G. F. Muntz also instigated the building of Umberslade Baptist church and adjoining school in 1876 and in 1892 the Institute, later renamed King George VI Memorial Hall, in memory of the late Mr Walter Higgs of Nuthurst Grange. In 1978 the hall was modernised, thanks to the generosity of the adjoining Men's Social Club, and is now run by this organisation.

In 1913 a new council school was built for 120 pupils, including those from the now closed Baptist school and school in School Road. In 1920 it became a central school and pupil teachers training college, drawing in children from a wide area of the surrounding countryside. It was extended in 1935 to accommodate infants. It is now a primary school with 140 pupils, who leave at the age of eleven years to go to schools in Solihull.

The foundation stone for St Thomas' church was laid in 1879 by Mr Thomas Burman of Warings Green, who was chief subscriber. Completed in 1880 at a cost of £2,500, it was dedicated to St Thomas as a compliment to Thomas Burman. The vicarage was built in 1896.

The sporting life of the village increased in the 1920s with the acquisition of land for recreation. This was due to the enterprise and generosity of Mr Harry Mould of Hockley House and grants from Warwickshire and National Playing Fields Associations, Carnegie Trustees and by money raising events. Several hundred pounds was raised by Mr Mould, who acquired a Rhode car, value £235, and took it around the country inviting people to subscribe one shilling to the Recreation Ground Fund. The car was raffled at a concert held at the Institute on 3rd November 1923.

Hockley Heath has a population of approximately 2,000 with a Parish Council and Residents Association, who jointly obtained the rebuilding recently of the pavilion on the recreation ground.

During the Second World War, land was commandeered to make an aerodrome for training glider pilots. A farmhouse was demolished, trees and hedges cleared, ponds and ditches filled in and part of Ashford Lane obliterated. The land has now reverted to private ownership.

For its size Hockley Heath is well endowed with pubs and eating places, a legacy from its coaching days. It has shops, post office, an assortment of commercial enterprises ranging from swimming pool and upholstery specialists to building and home suppliers, a timber merchant and large motor dealer. Gone are the old trades such as brickmaking, rakemaking, blacksmiths, cobblers and slaughterers, but bread is still baked at the bakery at Illshaw Heath, almost uninterrupted for the past 150 years at least. There was once a doctor's surgery and banking facilities several days a week. There is still a dental surgery in the village.

Despite its outwardly urban character, with its modern houses, there is much that is truly rural on its doorstep. Trees, flora and fauna abound in woods and fields. Agriculture is changing from small dairy farming to sheep and cereals, intensive poultry and egg production and horse riding stables.

Its position so near the heart of the Midland industrial conurbation means, inevitably, that Hockley Heath has become increasingly popular among commuters, especially since the building of the motorways north and south of the village.

Hurst Green ✑

Lying on the northern edge of the town of Halesowen, with its ancient abbey ruins and fine Norman church, Hurst Green remained for centuries a farming area with very few inhabitants.

Before the Norman conquest Halas had been part of the Clent Hundred. The first documented details of the area were recorded in the Domesday Book of 1086. The figures entered for Halas suggest that much development had occurred in the pre-conquest era.

The manor of Halas was given by King William to his friend Earl Roger de Montgomery of Shropshire. David ap Owyen, Prince of Wales, became lord of the manor by edict of Henry II in 1177 but it was not until 1271 that the suffix Owen was added to the manor's name. In 1214 it again changed hands, being granted by King John to the Bishop of Winchester to enable him to found a religious order. By 1218 an abbey had been constructed and the first members of the Premonstratensian monks arrived from Picardy. These were known as the 'White Canons' because of their flowing white robes and hoods, black being the more usual mode of attire. The monks remained at the abbey until its dissolution in 1538.

It was subsequently granted to Sir John Dudley, a favoured member of the court of Henry VIII, and eventually purchased by Sir John Lyttleton in 1560. It remains today in the hands of the Lyttleton family.

What is Hurst Green's place in this historic background? The translation of the name from the original Old English – 'trees on a hillock' – seems far removed from the spread of urban develop-

Hurst Green Methodist chapel

ment, the large housing estates, and the continuous roar of nearby motorway traffic of today. All that remains of the old farmsteads which dotted the landscape up to the turn of the century are their names. These are now found in the nomenclature of local roads eg Roundhills.

The oldest building in the area is Thatcher's Barn. Though in a state of disrepair, its old beams are still intact. It is said to date from Tudor times or even earlier. The rest of the farm has long since disappeared and the site is now occupied by a haulage firm.

A few hundred yards away a 200 year old cottage still stands. Its occupant remembers her grandfather making nails there. This was once a common home industry in which a whole family, including the children, were employed.

The Fairfield public house, with its inn sign clearly depicting a garish fairground scene of swings and roundabouts, is a reminder of the visits of Pat Collins' Funfair, which took place annually on the 'night soil' area immediately opposite.

Built before 1685, Cakemore Mansion in Masters Lane was another notable building in the parish. Really a large farmstead, its orchards provided apples for the making of cider in the Mansion House barns. It was demolished as recently as 1966. A new Liberal Club now stands on the site.

Cakemore Mansion had close connections with the Adams/ Attwood families whose coat of arms can be seen in Halesowen and Birmingham libraries. Ann Adams, daughter of the owner, was the mother of Thomas Attwood, who became well known for his work on Parliamentary Reform. He was one of Birmingham's first two MPs.

The Adams family were interested in education and opened one of the first Sunday schools in Worcestershire. This was founded in 1752 in Masters Lane. It offered the only source of learning in the district for the poorer classes. Adults and children both attended for lessons in reading and writing.

Religion has always played a large part in the lives of the inhabitants of Hurst Green. In 1529 the monks of Halas Abbey established a chapel at Oldbury. Prior to this, people wishing to worship had to make their way to Halesowen, crossing the dreary 'Bleak Heath' – 'a welter of floods and swamps' in winter and in rainy seasons. The name Cakemore, derived from 'Cacca's marshy land', can be traced back to documents as early as 1270.

Hurst Green Methodist church celebrated its Golden Jubilee in 1987. This is the third church to be built in an area to which John Wesley was a frequent visitor. The first was a small tin hut erected in Hurst Green Road as a shelter for itinerant preachers and their congregations. Services had earlier been conducted in the open around a roughly built stone altar. The second church was built in 1900 but by 1937 had become too small for the number of worshippers.

Hurst Green had a minor poet and artist, in the form of David Parkes. Born in Cakemore in 1763, he showed great talent for drawing from a very early age – scrawling in chalk on the doorstep of his father's cottage. Some of his original watercolours are now housed in the British Museum. His leisure time was spent in travel – making drawings of antiquities and amassing collections.

It is due to his endeavours that many silver and copper coins of Roman origin were discovered in Cakemore. One of these bore the head of Julia, daughter of Titus AD 40–81, and another that of Septimus Severus, a Roman Emperor who came to Britain in AD 208.

Keresley End 🌿

At the turn of the century, Keresley was a truly rural area of quiet beauty, with a few farmhouses dotted here and there, until rich seams of coal were discovered underground. A mine was sunk in 1911, known as Coventry Colliery, and the village of New Keresley was built to house the men seeking employment there. This covered an area from Old Keresley to the outskirts of Corley (where stands Corley Hall, which is mentioned in the novel *Adam Bede*, by George Eliot). The closeknit community which now exists has evolved from these men and their families.

In 1919, the Sankey Commission was set up for the welfare of mineworkers and their families. Among their recommendations were the building of a social club and sports facilities, and Keresley mineworkers and their families were some of the first beneficiaries. At the side of the social club there was a cricket field, football ground and bowling green which are still in use today. Tennis courts were laid out and also a lovely landscaped park with sunken gardens and a bandstand. For the children a large recreation ground was provided. Unfortunately, these are no longer there.

In 1931, Mrs Fenn, the colliery manager's wife, decided the miners wives needed an interest and a local Women's Institute was formed. During the Second World War the WI played their part by knitting for the troops, and canning and preserving fruit and vegetables. WI members were among those who offered accommodation to people who came into Keresley to escape the bombings of the City of Coventry. The village escaped lightly with the exception of a direct hit on Manor Farm, Keresley, which dates back to the 19th century.

Dating from the early days of the new mining village there are two churches; Congregational and Anglican. At this time there were a few shops, a post office and a general store on the main road.

The education of the village children, up to the age of eleven, was for two generations under the guidance of Mr Douce, a strict disciplinarian. From the age of eleven, the children travelled to Ash Green, a senior school about a mile away, until a senior school was built in the village. However, due to falling rolls the senior school has been closed.

On the edge of the village is an area of outstanding natural beauty – Bunsons Wood – and people from near and far come to see the magnificent carpet of bluebells which herald the coming of spring each year.

In recent years there have been many changes, but it is still basically a mining village. Starting in 1953, about 500 more houses were built to provide accommodation for the miners who were recruited because of the expansion of the mine. Around the same time, approximately 80 council houses were also built, and the council provided new play areas and additional sports facilities (including a pavilion) near to this new estate, next to the only village pub, the Golden Eagle. Part of this development was the provision of eight shops in a small precinct which are still serving the village today.

Newlands House, formerly the colliery manager's house, is now a home for the elderly, and more elderly people are cared for in a new sheltered housing complex, Alwynne Freeman Court in the heart of the village. There have for many years been thriving Darby and Joan Clubs, the highlight of which are the annual Christmas parties.

On the doorstep is the huge Homefire Plant which provides employment for local people. However, it is a constant source of complaint from local residents, due to its smoke and fall-out of black dust over a wide area. The Parish Council, over a long period of time, have fought to have this problem alleviated and it hopes to find a solution in the near future.

A very successful carnival and fair was organised in 1988. This was for the first time since the miners' strike of 1984, reviving an annual village tradition. This has helped a little to heal the wounds and restore the community spirit, which was deeply affected during the miners' strike.

Many miners and council tenants have been able to buy their houses, and this has dramatically altered the appearance of the village with individual modernisation of properties. The effect of the development of a new private housing estate on the site of the old senior school, is yet to be seen.

It would seem that Keresley End (as the village is now called) will continue to change, but the community spirit will still, hopefully remain.

Keresley Heath

Keresley is not mentioned in the Domesday Book but is first documented early in the 12th century when Earl Ranulph de Gernon gave a chapelry there to the Benedictine priory in Coventry. Later in the same century Earl de Blundeville gave the priory an area of wood and waste.

The name Keresley is thought to be of Anglo-Saxon Danish origin. The civil parish is roughly in the shape of a long triangle, with the wider end running north to the higher land of Corley and the southern point pushing into the city of Coventry. In early times it was an outlying part of the parish of St Michael in the city.

Keresley Heath, in the south of the parish, grew during the late 18th century, in the angle between the ancient trackways, Astley way (later Bennetts Lane, now Bennetts Road) and Corley way (now Tamworth Road). Tamworth Road was turnpiked in 1762 to facilitate the carrying of coal from the north into Coventry, where it was sold for 4d per hundredweight as against 7d for coal from Bedworth. The increase in traffic no doubt encouraged the growth of the village. In some medieval documents the name Keresley is spelled 'Carsley' or 'Karsley' and so it is pronounced today by members of old-established families.

In pre-Reformation days the spiritual care of the people was in the hands of a Benedictine monk, whose dwelling was in Sandpits Lane where Akon House, a timber-framed 17th century farmhouse, still stands. Ancient stone-work dug up in the garden may be all that remains of the chapel.

In 1842 it was decided to build a parish church and one of the leading architects of the time, Benjamin Ferry, FSA, FRIBA, was engaged. The edifice, of local sandstone, cost £3,000. It was consecrated in 1847 as the church of St Thomas, parish church of Keresley with Coundon. It stands to the west of the village on the boundary with Coundon.

The first vicar was the Rev W. H. Thickens, who lived in some state in Keresley House about a mile and a half away on Tamworth Road near the border of Corley. He presented scarlet cloaks to the old women and purple frocks to the girls of the parish, to be worn when they attended church. They must have made a brave show in the elegant new building. When the vicar died, his body was carried through the grounds of his house and along the road to the church between lines of his grieving parishioners.

The High Street runs east to west from Bennetts Road to Tamworth Road, thus cutting off the point of the angle between the main roads. This grassy area was the common and it is believed that in days long past, the gallows stood here. In 1852 a National school was built on the common and drew pupils from a wide area as it was the only school in the district. New Road was cut through from Bennetts Road to Tamworth Road, running roughly parallel with the High Street. By the end of the century, an infants school had been erected on the east side of Bennetts Road. The National school was demolished in the 1960s after standing empty for a long time. The infants school is now unused and presents a sad sight with its windows boarded. A big Roman Catholic comprehensive school has been built in Sandpits Lane, its grounds and playing fields stretching up to the church.

In 1920 Keresley and Coundon Women's Institute, with valuable local help, built a hall known for the 50 years of its life as 'the Institute'. It became the focal point for most of the social life of the village. In 1970 a church hall was built, taking over to a great extent the role of the old Institute.

In the 18th century much of the convivial life of the village must have centred in and around the inn, the Shepherd and Shepherdess. In 1790, so the Coventry Leet Book tells us, three men, Farnsworth, Phillips and Archer were hanged for committing burglary there. Later, the Bell Inn was built on the corner of Bennetts Road and the High Street. The original inns have long gone but the public houses erected in their places have kept the old names.

From earliest days, when the Keresley inhabitants scratched a living from their little clearings in the forest, until well into this century, the area was rural and agricultural. Even now, the two main roads, after leaving the village, run between hedges and fields. Early in the 19th century Coventry's ribbon-weaving industry, introduced perhaps by Huguenots fleeing religious persecution, was employing 10,000 workers, both men and women, including the majority of the wage earners in Keresley Heath. Later, many of the village women made a little money by doing bead-work and making other trimmings for the elaborate dresses of the wives of Coventry's up-and-coming industrialists. When this trade fell away the women turned to laundry-work for the big houses which were appearing in the area.

In 1911 a coal mine was developed in the fields lying beyond the hamlet of Keresley Green and this provided a variety of better paid jobs for the local men.

Between the world wars, Coventry's great industrial expansion in the manufacture of bicycles, then cars and finally aircraft, brought prosperity, and an influx of workers, to the whole area, including Keresley Heath. While the villagers were commuting daily, mainly by bicycle, to work in the city, the city was moving northward to engulf their village and turn them into suburbanites.

The interest of rich Coventry citizens in the potential of the Keresley area appears as early as the 14th century when two city butchers acquired land there for the grazing of cattle. By the 19th century, the successful industrialists were looking at the high airy land of the parish as a more salubrious place to build their fine houses than the cramped streets of the city. The New House, later renamed the Moat House, after passing through the hands of several owners, became the home of the Cash family. Sidney Cash managed the world famous ribbon-weaving firm of J and J Cash. Christopher Cash invented the captive bolt, a humane-killer to be used in abattoirs.

On Tamworth Road were built the houses of William Hillman of the Hillman Motor Company and of Sir John Black of Standard Motors. The Hillman property, after serving as a war-time hospital, is now the Royal Court Hotel. Sir John Black's house has been demolished.

A Keresley resident with a less well known name was Mr Bertie Statham, a boot and shoe maker who patented a football boot stud which was used by leading clubs throughout England. His son was a motor-cyclist of international fame.

King's Heath 🦋

Although King's Heath is now a thriving residential suburb of Birmingham, approximately four miles south from the city centre, it was once just what the name implies, a heath (in Worcestershire) belonging to the king. The first recorded name of 'Kyngesheth' appeared in a deed dated 1541.

In 1772 an Act of Parliament led to its first development. All waste and common land had to be enclosed and accounted for. Then when the main turnpike road from Birmingham to Spemall Ash was opened, it crossed the heath and a few cottages were built, mainly near the toll gate. You could not reach King's Heath from Birmingham without paying several tolls. This is the Alcester Road we know today.

Two of these original cottages were joined together to make the first inn, and as the landlord was a gunsmith, he called it The Cross Guns. The only other inn was The Kings Arms, further along the road at what is now Alcester Lanes End. Both of these establishments are still flourishing today. One unusual use of these premises was to act as a courtroom and records show that it was quite a common sight to see local 'wrongdoers' chained to the fireplace awaiting transportation to less comfortable surroundings. A licence was granted to the landlord of the Cross Guns in 1831. He brewed his own beer, which later led to a large brewery being built at the rear of the inn. It was demolished at the beginning of the 20th century when a large corporation took over the management of the inn.

King's Heath had two policemen at this period and they had their headquarters at the corner of what is now York Road – with the stocks opposite. Their station was rebuilt in Silver Street, before being rebuilt and enlarged on its present site in the High Street of today.

The largest house in the district at the end of the 18th century was a mansion called The Grange. This was built in parkland of 350 acres in the area 200 yards west of the turnpike road and 450 yards north of Bleak Lane (later renamed Vicarage Road). When the Gloucester to Birmingham railway was built in 1840 this estate was split into two halves. The Grange was finally demolished in

1895 and the land developed into highly desirable building plots – hence today's road names of Grange Road, Avenue Road etc.

The opening of the railway station at King's Heath brought many people to the area and when the steam tramcar from Birmingham was introduced, the High Street grew. By the year 1891 the population had reached almost 5,000. Large houses built in the area included The Priory (near King Edward's school in Vicarage Road) for the Cartland family – hence Cartland Road; Highbury (in Highbury Park, via Yew Tree Road), home of Joseph Chamberlain MP; and Uffculme (in Queensbridge Road) for the Cadbury family. It is interesting to note that all these houses were built near the railway, all to the west of the main road. Some land was developed to the east of the main road on Mr Valentine's land (hence Valentine Road) but the 'gentry' favoured the west side.

The first religious house 'opened' was the Baptist chapel in the High Street in 1816, then the Church of England built All Saint's in 1860. The Wesleyan chapel was built in 1887 and St Dunstan's Roman Catholic church in 1896 (in Station Road).

Education was provided by the various churches and other organisations. The King's Heath National school was opened in 1846, the primary school in 1878 and adult education was catered for by the Moseley and King's Heath Institute in 1878. This was built on the corner of High Street and Institute Road (now Woolworth's corner).

King's Heath became a suburb of Birmingham in 1911 and expanded towards the west in the Dad's Lane area around 1925.

Leisure interests were provided by opening the public library in 1903, the swimming baths in 1924 and later the Kingsway and Ideal cinemas and the greyhound stadium.

Today King's Heath has a very busy High Street. Most of the well known modern supermarkets and shops can be found, although it does still retain its strong village identity.

The most modern leisure centre has been opened at Cock's Moor's Woods Golf Course and a new community centre in Heathfield Road. There is still very little industry in King's Heath, and it remains mostly a mixed residential area.

King's Norton 🥀

The old village of King's Norton is today a thriving suburb of Birmingham, lying four or five miles from the city centre. A dense network of roads contains residential and industrial sites, with a village green at the centre, an ancient parish church and a park, while a busy dual carriageway leads to the railway station and the secondary centre of Cotteridge.

'Probably no part of the Greater Birmingham area is richer in historical association than King's Norton and Northfield'. So says Arthur Lock in his history of the district. The area was only sparsely populated at first because of the dense forest; the Celts were the first inhabitants – Lickey is a Celtic name – then the Romans came in AD43. They built two roads which intersected, probably at the river Rea. Icknield Street ran from Cirencester through Alcester, Studley and Beoley to Lifford, entering Stirchley Street at Breedon Cross and going on to Birmingham; the Saltway, as its name implies, was built to carry salt from Droitwich through Bromsgrove, Selly Oak, Saltley and Salter's Croft (near Tamworth) to Saltfleet on the Lincolnshire coast en route to the continent. When a house was demolished on Bristol Road to make way for the tramway extension to the Lickey Hills, part of a Roman aqueduct and some Roman coins were found. When the Ice Age glaciers retreated, large deposits of clay were left in the King's Norton area which were used by the Romans to make pottery and bricks, and fragments of these have been found. Enough was left in the 19th century for a brickworks to be sited there.

The court of the manor of Bromsgrove was held at Lickey. It regulated the enforcement of labour, food and drink prices, awarding punishment for trespass, false weights and measures etc. King's Norton became a separate manor during Queen Elizabeth's reign and its court was held locally until 1876, but by that time it had become no more than an excuse for a dinner at the Fighting Cocks inn in Moseley – another of the berewicks of Bromsgrove.

King's Norton belonged to the King from the Norman Conquest until the reign of Henry III, then again from Edward IV until 1804. During the interval came the rise and fall of the Mortimers. A

Roger Mortimer was awarded £100 from the manor for rescuing Edward I from imprisonment in Hereford Castle. In 1317 Edward II granted the manor to John Mortimer. Edward III was much influenced by Roger Mortimer until the latter, in 1330, was arraigned for the murder of Edward II and hanged. Nonetheless, the land was restored to the Mortimer family in 1354.

In the 16th century John Leland passed through and described 'Norton' as a 'pretty uplandish town in Worcs. There be some fayre housys of staplears that use to by wolle and also a fair church and a goodly piramus of stone over the bellframe. There runneth a little brooke at the west end of the town, good plenty of wood and pasture and meetly good corne betwixt Alchurch and Norton and likewise between Norton and Bermingham toon that be distant about five miles'. By Elizabeth's time, Feckenham Forest had largely disappeared, burnt to make salt at Droitwich. Many fine houses which were built in the 16th and 17th centuries still stand, including Primrose Hill Farm, Lifford Hall, Bells Farm, Monyhull Hall and Brandwood House.

During the Civil War, King's Norton belonged to Henrietta Maria, the wife of Charles I. The year after the 'skirmish' between Prince Rupert and Lord Willoughby at King's Norton, which Willoughby won, the Queen marched to join her husband, arriving at 'her own manor' with 3,000 horsemen, 30 companies of foot soldiers, a train of artillery and a long line of baggage wagons! They camped around the village while the Queen lodged at the bailiff's house now known as the Saracen's Head. It became one of the many public houses round the green but was later given by the brewery to be a church hall as it stands next to the church. (There is now another church hall).

A charter was granted in 1616, for the right to hold a market and two fairs. These fairs finished at the end of the 19th century and all that remains is the October 'Mop' – so called as it was originally a hiring fair. In the 17th and 18th centuries, many trades and industries were listed in the village, among them nailers, wheelwrights, brickmakers, weavers and tanners, though previously the area had been mainly agricultural. The old cottages which clustered round the green survived until 1936, when Birmingham Council destroyed a part of the village's history. One building, now housing a shop on the ground floor, is known to

93

have its origins in the 15th century and still has well preserved old timbers and many fine features.

King's Norton's fortunes varied with those of the great families who lived within its boundaries, the Mortimers, Grevises, Haukeslawes, Jervoys, Jolliffes, Liffords, Littletons, Middlemores and Pountneys. The Sparrings of Monyhull, with others, lost their houses because of their involvement in the Gunpowder Plot. In 1908, Monyhull Hall, by then the property of Birmingham Corporation, became a colony for 1,000 'epileptic and mentally defective folk', setting, by its successful example, a model for many similar institutions.

North of the green stands the church of St Nicholas. The earliest part of the church is Norman and there are two small round-headed windows in the north wall of the chancel, though not in their original position. Records show that the church was 'enlarged by the monks of Worcester' in the 13th century.

During the Civil War, lead from the roof was stripped and used to make bullets, altars and images removed and the high altar replaced with a plain wooden table. Much was replaced at the Restoration and again in the 18th century various alterations and additions were made. Further restoration took place during the Victorian era and many gifts were donated – a replacement organ, a brass eagle lectern, a font and a clock for the tower among others. A new vestry was built to commemorate the Jubilee of Queen Victoria. In 1950 more restoration and refurbishment took place and monies were raised in 1953 to make the fabric of the church safe.

The church houses many old fine tombs and monuments, though some of them are hidden from view. The oldest is a tomb to Humphrey Toye, 1514, under the floor of the Lady Chapel. Under the bell tower are two large tombs. One, a 15th century marble altar tomb, is for Humphrey Littleton and Martha his wife, but the tomb only holds Martha, as Humphrey was buried at Naunton Beauchamp ... we can only wonder why. The other, most elaborate, tomb is that of Sir Richard Grevis and his wife Dame Anne. The two figures on the tomb are recumbent and beautifully portrayed in 17th century dress. Above the figures is a long verse extolling Sir Richard's many virtues, and their eight children are also shown.

By the north door is a small inscription set in the wall, telling the sad fate of William Greves:-

The ascension day of the ninth of May
Third year of King James raigne,
I, William Greves was slain,
To end my tyme and steal my coyne,
I, William Greves was slain.   1605.

It is said that this man was a tax collector who lived in a cottage on Parsons Hill. The culprit was never brought to justice, as there was the added complication that three men with the same name as the accused lived in the parish. Many tombs in the churchyard bear the names of old families who have lived in King's Norton over the centuries.

In the north-east corner of the churchyard stands a building known as the Old Grammar School. This building is most unusual because the upper storey is older than the lower. The upper storey was most probably originally built on stilts in the 15th century and the lower underbuilt in Elizabethan times, as the doorway clearly shows. Inside, the upper storey displays many fine beams and a most unusual wooden tracery window.

It is said that this was a King Edward VI school, but this is not so, as when Edward's commissioners surveyed the school, it was reported that 'a scole had always been kept there'.

At the beginning of the 17th century, Tobias Gyles, 'a graceless dominie', was master. After three years, and being found neglectful of his duties, local people sought to get him dismissed. After a great deal of argument and even complaints to the Lord Treasurer, Gyles lost his mastership. He still retained his curacy but that too ended when he performed an illegal marriage between two local people.

He was followed in 1629 by Thomas Hall, the school's most brilliant and distinguished master. Hall was only 19 at the time of his appointment but nevertheless, attracted pupils from far and wide, the Midlands, Northumberland and even Ireland. He sent his better pupils to universities and even some to the Puritan New Hall Inn at Oxford. Hall himself was a Presbyterian whose sympathies lay with the Parliamentarians. During the Civil War he was often accused, cursed, threatened with death, plundered and five times imprisoned. He wrote many books and treatises, among the latter 'The loathsomeness of long hair', 'Painting of spots and naked breasts ... to enflame lusts in the hearts of men', and also a diatribe against maypoles.

At the time of the Restoration, Hall started to write his auto-biography, his will and a catalogue of his many books. He decreed that 750 books were to go to ministers at King's Norton, Moseley and Wythall, 300 of his 'best books' to Birmingham as a minis-terial library, and 270 'schoole books and phylogophy' were for King's Norton. A collection of Hall's books is now housed in Birmingham Central Library.

The year 1662 saw the ejection of Hall from the ministry as he would not subscribe to the Act of Uniformity. He defied the law by not leaving the parish and eventually died of 'a broken heart' on 13th April 1665 at 4.00 pm. He was buried, by his own wish, amongst 'the common people' and his grave is unknown.

Various masters followed, though none had his brilliance, en-thusiasm and erudition. Over the years the school declined until the founding of the Board School in 1876. The Old Grammar School fell into neglect, despite repairs made in 1909 – 1910, when a new external staircase was added. A few years later the Charity Commissioners sold the building for £10 to Theodore Pritchett, who gave it to St Nicholas' church. During the Second World War, it was again neglected and vandalised but was re-stored in 1951 with a generous grant from the Pilgrim Trust. Today, the building is used by the choir and stands as a perpetual memorial to one of the older grammar schools in the Midlands and to its most revered master, Thomas Hall.

As the Industrial Revolution gained momentum, Birmingham expanded and 'manufactories' came to King's Norton because land was cheaper. Barbara Cartland's grandfather established his works there and her brother Ronald was MP for King's Norton during the 1930s, much loved for his work for the unemployed. He was killed at Dunkirk in 1940 in the Second World War.

In 1846, King's Norton became a separate parish from Broms-grove: the population was expanding rapidly from the 1841 census figure of 5,500. Among the trades, nailers, brickmakers, wheelwrights and tanners are mentioned.

In 1911, King's Norton had its own mint and in 1918/19 coins were marked 'KN'. The Metal Co eventually became part of ICI.

The Worcester Canal was opened only after 24 years of work, because of difficulties of terrain, the worst being the two mile tunnel at King's Norton. The railway however, soon proved a more successful form of travel. Because of good transport, many large factories opened, among them Cadbury's, Bournville becoming a separate village in 1900.

With the passing of the Greater Birmingham Extension Act in 1911, all of King's Norton, except for Wythall and part of Rednal, was absorbed into the city. Now it is a popular suburb, still with its village green, bordered by the church, the Saracen's Head and the ancient grammar school. Some pleasant flats have replaced the old cinema and the only remaining public house is the Bull. The library was funded from the Carnegie Trust and there are separate boys and girls secondary schools, the former a direct descendant of the old grammar school. At the 1981 census, the population numbered 24,548, for an area smaller than that used for the 1841 count.

Knowle

Although, these days, Knowle is generally regarded as a town, to the older residents it is still 'the village'. The name comes from the Saxon, and means a small hill.

It is first recorded in about 1200, when William de Arden conveyed a grant of dower to his wife Amice de Traci. Knowle became a Royal manor in 1285 when the de Arden family sold the manor to King Edward I and Queen Eleanor. After her death the King gave the manor to the Abbots and Priors of Westminster. It has, since then, passed through many hands.

In 1396 Knowle's first and greatest benefactor, Walter Cook, applied for a faculty to build a chapel on land owned by his parents. At this time villagers had to journey to Hampton-in-Arden, the parent manor and parish. This meant crossing the river Blythe at Eastcote by a ford which, when in flood, was often a great hazard. The faculty obtained from the Pope, the church was built and in 1402 consecrated by the Bishop of Dunkeld, Perth-shire. Walter Cook died in 1423 and was buried in his chapel.

In 1547, at the time of the Dissolution of the Monasteries, it was thanks to 'that great and daungerous water', the Blythe, that the church was saved from destruction.

The Guild House, one of Knowle's architectural gems, was built in 1412. It was then the home of the Guild of St Anne of Knowle. During its lifetime it has had several uses including, at one time, as a Post Office, then a draper's and newsagent's. In 1911 it was sold to Mr G. Jackson, who had it restored and gave it back to the church. Another of Knowle's proud possessions is Grimshaw Hall, visited in 1927 by HM Queen Mary.

A weekly market used to be held at the back of the High Street, where it was possible to buy anything from a bag of apples to an antique sideboard.

In the 18th century, the poet Walter Savage Landor was a boarder at a school in Knowle before going to Rugby.

Longdon Hall, which stood on land now part of the golf course, was at one time owned by Lady Byron. Fulke Greville, 5th Lord Brook and lord of the manor, was in residence there for a while in 1682.

In 1749 the village was visited by John Wesley, who preached in the Red Lion yard. He was not very impressed with Knowle or its inhabitants!

There have been many changes in the village since the end of the Second World War. Open spaces in and around the centre have been built on, cottages in the High Street demolished and shops and offices erected on the sites. The cinema, which stood in Station Road, was knocked down and a garage built. A supermarket was opened and the smaller grocery shops, which had served the population for years, closed. A high school was built and then a new infants and junior school. The old school in Kenilworth Road became, eventually, flatlets for the elderly. The police station was moved to a new site and then closed down, the building then became the new home for the doctors' surgery.

Knowle Society and the Women's Institute now keep 'an eagle eye' on development plans and attempt to preserve that village atmosphere which still prevails despite modernisation.

Lode Heath 🌿

Lode is a contraction of 'Leewode' (first recorded in 1344) and means 'a sheltered wood'. 'Leewode Heth', adjoining the wood, was an extensive area of open heathland situated on the east side of Lode Lane, approximately between Grove Road and Moat Lane. Lode Lane ran from the present Warwick Road to the Coventry Road, winding its way across the heath.

The whole area was once part of the Forest of Arden. A majestic reminder is the Spanish chestnut tree standing some 150 yards across Lode Lane from St Ninian's church. This tree is said to be about 700 years old. Wherever the soil was clay there was thick deciduous forest but there were areas of light sandy soil where tree growth was not so dense and which, therefore, facilitated easier clearance. These areas became heath lands and one of these was Leewode Heth, which over the years became known as Lode Heath. It is now a suburb of Solihull.

The Great Western Railway station was opened in Solihull in 1852 (Birmingham to Paddington line) and this precipitated a gradual change in Solihull, which until this time was a quiet semi-rural village. Even today some of the older inhabitants of the area still refer to Solihull as 'the village'. Around the 1850s many large middle class families, earning comfortable incomes from industry and investments, realised the quality of life offered in the Solihull area was very attractive and built large villas, several of which were located in Lode Lane.

The edition of the Ordnance Survey Map published in 1886 shows that several houses and farms had appeared in the Lode Heath area, one of which was The Grove on the corner of Grove Road. This is now a residence for the elderly. There is still a cottage in Grove Road, overlooking Solihull school sports field, called Lode Heath Cottage. This could well be one of the cottages marked on the same map.

The Hermitage, another large house on Lode Lane, was originally built in 1869 by the Rev Charles Evans, a headmaster of King Edward School, Birmingham, and later rector of Solihull. In April 1905 the house was badly damaged by fire but it was restored in 1915 and used by the Red Cross as a hospital for war wounded until 1919. In 1920 it was acquired by the Local Authority as a childrens home. This was eventually closed in the late 1970s and the house and surrounding area is now a development of flats and bungalows for the elderly.

It also appears from old maps that there was a windmill almost opposite The Hermitage built by 1787 which ceased working in the early 19th century. Another place of interest is the Mill Pool in Lode Lane. At the end of the 18th century a mill was fed by this pool and worked until 1904. The mill buildings were demolished and a large housing estate now covers the site. The pool and woods that encircle it are now an area of considerable wild life. It often echoes with the sound of young voices as a group of Solihull Scouts have their headquarters nearby.

The Warwick to Birmingham Canal runs through this area and was opened in the 1790s. There was a wharf at Lode Heath from where coal, building materials, ironware and imported foodstuffs were exchanged for agricultural produce, including, no doubt, flour from the nearby mill. Many a good ale must have been supped at the nearby Anchor Inn, of which nothing now remains.

Also in the 1860s the first gas works was opened and this supplied gas initially for street lighting and eventually domestic lighting, which meant the end of paraffin lamps lighting many a Lode Heath home.

Coming more up to date, there is a large house opposite The Hermitage; this was built in the 1920s on the site of Ramby House. During the Second World War the Norwegian Consul occupied this house but since the 1950s it has been a dental surgery.

Gradually the area developed with the growth of industry and one of the main employers has been the Rover Company. In 1939 the Air Ministry planned to build a factory, initially to manufacture components for the Bristol Hercules radial aircraft engine. This factory was under the control of the Rover Company and met originally with considerable local opposition. However, the first complete Rover-built engine was finished and tested by October, 1940. The factory continued on this basis throughout the Second World War, but was eventually handed over to the Rover Car Company at an official opening by the then President of the Board of Trade, Sir Stafford Cripps, on 2nd February, 1946. It became Land Rover Co in 1978 and now employs some 8,500 people.

The general growth of industry led to the development of large residential areas, both private and municipal. As in the past the area is still attractive to families working in Birmingham but, with the opening of new motorways and improved rail links, commuting to business centres including London is not uncommon.

The community is well served by schools ranging from nursery education through to 16 year olds. Lode Heath school was opened in 1938 and it was from this school that the first pupils for the newly formed grammar schools were selected. Mr Arthur Lunnon was headmaster at this time.

Good medical care is available in the locality with several group practice facilities. The local hospital is on the site of the old Solihull Union workhouse and part of the original building is still in use.

Marston Green

Marston Green was originally known as 'Merstone Culy', but had assumed the name of Marston Green by 1882. It is thought Marston Green was probably the 'Merstone' described in the Domesday Book of 1086.

The Ordnance Survey map of 1886 shows Marston Green as a small village with a chapel, school, post office and a railway station, a public house and several scattered houses and farms, some of which were Elizabethan.

All this has changed now. The original public house is now known as Ash Tree Cottage, situated in Station Road near the junction with Coleshill Road. The present tavern was built on a site in Station Road near the junction with Alcott Lane. This is the second public house to be built on this site, the former one being demolished to allow the widening of Alcott Lane.

The old school and the adjoining schoolhouse where the headmaster lived have both gone and a library and clinic have taken their place. The children of infant and junior school age are now taught in separate modern purpose-built schools in the centre of the village.

After the First World War it was thought there should be a memorial to the fallen. After a great deal of controversy it was decided to build a village hall. This was of wooden structure, but it served the social life of the village very well. This has now been replaced by a larger brick built village hall on the same site. The memorials to both wars are permanently installed in the Garden of Memory, a wedge-shaped green at the heart of the village that was once a gravel pit. There are stone tablets in the garden giving the names of 13 men lost during the First World War and, by coincidence, 13 killed during the Second World War.

The old Cottage Homes built around the turn of the century is now known as Chelmsley Hospital. Adjoining this hospital during the Second World War, a hospital was built for use by wounded Canadians, now Marston Green Maternity Hospital.

The religious needs of the village are met by St Leonard's church and the free church.

Marston Green, from being a small isolated agricultural village, now adjoins Birmingham and is surrounded on one side by the huge Chelmsley Wood Estate which is an overspill estate for Birmingham Corporation. The name derives from Chelmsley Wood, which in earlier days was carpeted with bluebells and had many rhododendron bushes. Adjoining this at the eastern end of the village a 200 acre Business Park is being constructed. Coming round to the south-east side, there is the huge National Exhibition Centre and international railway station with their extensive car parks. Adjoining these coming towards the south is the new airport terminal serving Birmingham Airport, which stretches all along the western side of the village, the taxi-way being very close to those houses built along the western edge of the village. All this development has of course resulted in the demolition of the old farms and their cottages on these sites.

Meriden

The road from the east into Meriden descends a long steep hill, which was notorious and dangerous until the great engineer Telford improved it, by cutting through the top and making an embankment at the bottom.

Halfway down the hill on the right hand side is the old road, which runs past the Queen's Head public house, with the 'Cooper-

The old market cross at Meriden, said to mark the centre of England

age' and 'Malt House' nearby where the barrels and beer were once made.

On the left hand side of Meriden Hill, a quarter of a mile up Church Lane, stands the ancient church of St Lawrence, surrounded by several interesting large properties. Moathouse Farm, a timber-framed building, is dated 1609 but is thought to be much older. This area around the church was the original village, and was called 'Alspathe' in the Domesday Book and until the time of Henry VI. From then on, the name 'Myreden' was used, and later, Meriden. The church was built by Lady Godiva, wife of Earl Leofric, who owned Alspathe in the time of Edward the Confessor.

A short way from the church is a well, in which, it is believed, St Lawrence baptised the first converts of the parish.

Meriden developed alongside the track in the valley, and became a staging post of some importance as the road was improved and the coaches from London to Holyhead used it.

At one time there were seven inns in the village and three blacksmiths, besides accommodation for travellers. The most famous hotel was The Bull's Head, which stood opposite the present village pool. Princess Victoria is said to have stopped here in 1832.

Most of the old properties have now gone, but a few remain on the Main Road. One is the Stone House, a sandstone building which was once the village lock-up. Although it is now two properties, the 'cell' still remains between the two front doors, small and windowless. It is to this house each year that swifts return to nest in the eaves.

Another old house is the 'Nags Head', a one-time coaching house, which is now a private home of much character and old world charm. The white timbered cottages along the road are named 'Waterfall Cottages' after a small waterfall that was opposite them at one time. This is where steam wagons would replenish their water tanks.

At the bottom of the hill is the old Church of England school house, now used as the doctors' surgery, and adjacent to it in the playground is the village hall and scout hut. A magnificent chestnut tree stands in the playground here.

Along the road, the Manor Hotel has an interesting history. This Georgian house used to be a brass foundry and the fine lectern in the church was made there.

Another Georgian house of note is Meriden Hall, now divided into flats. It stands on higher ground on the left of Main Road, looking down to a lake and coppice of old trees.

The shops of Meriden are alongside the green and here is the old market cross, said to mark the centre of England. At the opposite end of the green stands the Cyclists National Memorial, erected to the memory of cyclists who died in the two World Wars. This memorial is the scene of an annual service of remembrance, which is attended by cyclists from all parts of the British Isles on the nearest Sunday to 22nd May.

Several roads radiate from the green. The straight mile towards Hampton-in-Arden was built across Meriden Heath when the Enclosures Act came into being. The heath later became a race course and is now the North Warwickshire nine-hole golf course.

Alongside the Birmingham road, on the west side of the village, is fine old meadowland surrounded by old oaks. This is the home ground of the 'Woodmen of Arden' – one of the British Societies of Archers still shooting with the six foot longbow as used at Agincourt. Here is the 'Forest Hall', which houses ballroom, banqueting hall, kitchens and dressing rooms. Around the walls of the main room are the tall narrow lockers for each archer to house his long bows and arrows. These bows and arrows are still made by a local craftsman in the workshop in the forest grounds. Deposited in the Forest Hall is a horn said to have been used by Robin Hood, who according to tradition competed at the grounds.

Another society of archers in Britain is the Queen's Bodyguard of Scotland, the Royal Company of Archers from Edinburgh, and every three years these two societies compete for the Scotch Cup, the Woodmen of Arden wearing their Lincoln Green jackets.

Meriden, situated as it is between Coventry and Birmingham, is jealously guarding its green belt land and only infilling has been allowed.

From the village there are many pleasant walks, particularly on the high ground which runs from north and south.

Monkspath ✑

The first recorded mention of Monkspath is in 1153, when it was called 'Munchespathe'. Roger de Ulehale of Tanworth was granted the manor and the adjoining lands by William de Beaumont, the third Earl of Warwick.

A collection of 13th and 14th century deeds show that Shelley, which adjoins Monkspath, was a thriving settlement at that time, and traffic between Solihull and Henley-in-Arden passed through regularly as Shelley Lane was part of the King's highway. The road went via Church Hill, Hillfield, Shelley Lane and Shuttecotte Lane, joining the Stratford Road at Monkspath Bridge. The bridge, probably a foot bridge only, is first recorded in 1339. Previously there was a ford and the route from here was direct to Henley.

The land was first farmed communally, in strips, but later it was enclosed and divided into farms. The probable evidence of open fields, in the form of ridge and furrow, was still to be seen on Graves Shelley field in the 1960s.

Hay Lane was also an ancient roadway, making a crossroads with Shelley Lane. From 1332 there was a Smith's Pond at Shelley, created by John Fabro Smith of Monkspath. Commercial fish ponds were a thriving business in the medieval period when the church decreed so many meatless days. The pool changed hands frequently and was a valuable property and its banks were still clearly visible in the 1970s.

There is little mention of Monkspath and Shelley in the 17th and 18th centuries, although it is known that in 1789 Shelley Farm was occupied by William Smith and owned by Mr Short. The Rate Book of 1806 records William Harding as the owner and William Smith still being the occupant.

About 1820 many of the roads were closed as the traffic through them became less and they lacked importance. In the 1930s a row of semi-detached houses was built in Hay Lane and further houses and several businesses on the Stratford Road at Monkspath, including a garden centre.

Monkspath is now a large housing estate or mini-town. Shelley Farm has been converted to an attractive public house and once again Shelley is a thriving community.

One resident remembers Monkspath in the 1950s, when Hay Lane was the local 'tip'. 'You were in constant danger of being engulfed by other people's rubbish as you hurled your own rubbish on top of the heap. On rainy days 'wellies' were a must and you returned home with your car looking as if it had been on a safari. Looking at the present day landscape it is hard to believe what it once was'.

Members of Warwickshire Nature Conservation Trust have saved a meadow in Monkspath, reputed to have remained in its original state without being mown or ploughed for 200 years. The turf containing hundreds of rare wild plants has been carefully transplanted to a secret site in Temple Balsall five miles away. Tesco, the supermarket chain, donated £27,500 towards the cost of the removal and the land is now Tesco's local supermarket car park.

There is still a lot of development in progress at Monkspath including the rebuilding of Monkspath Hall, which was knocked down in error in 1980. The plans for the reinstatement of the Hall to its original form as a private dwelling house have been given the go-ahead, but as the original building was Queen Anne with Georgian alterations and Victorian additions this will not be an easy task!

Moseley

Moseley developed as a tiny settlement on a gravel bank between the rivers Cole and Rea, and had good spring water. The inhabitants were small farmers and their dependants. A few families became prosperous over the years, but the only name which comes down to us from the 15th century is that of Grevis, pronounced Greaves. Their tombs are still to be seen at nearby King's Norton. The villagers had to travel five miles for weddings, funerals etc and this led to the building of a small chapel at Moseley, its tower being completed in 1549. This building was added to piecemeal until 1900, when most of it was pulled down and rebuilt; only the tower of the old building remains.

Sir Richard Grevis was knighted by James I, and honours were heaped on him, including Sheriff of Worcestershire and Deputy Lieutenant of Wales. The family became very prosperous and lived in Moseley Hall. The exact situation of the original Hall is unknown, but at least one rebuilding took place during the 18th century at the site of the present Hall. The family fell on hard times, however, and their wealth dwindled away until the position was reached when the whole estate had to be sold to pay the family's debts, and in 1767 the Hall and Park were sold to John Taylor, who had made a fortune in Birmingham from the manufacture of buttons, snuffboxes, etc. He rebuilt the Hall as a fine stone mansion on its present site, and the grounds included fishponds, an ice house and a dovecote. These features still survive, but the Hall was badly damaged in the Priestley Riots of 1791. John Taylor's son rebuilt the mansion in 1796, and this is the building we see today. The family sold out in 1891 to Richard Cadbury, who presented the Hall to the City as a children's convalescent home. It is now a hospital for severely handicapped and geriatric patients.

In 1800 the village had a population of 400. These were in the main farm labourers, blacksmiths, nailers, grooms, and the out-

Part of Moseley village centre

side staff of Moseley Hall. Very few houses survive from this period. The two public houses, the Fighting Cocks and the down-market Bull's Head, were connected by the Birmingham to Alcester turnpike, laid out in 1801. A tollgate existed at the top of the hill. The six-horse stage coach paid one shilling toll here and stopped at the Fighting Cocks for refreshment and to pick up passengers. Before 1801 the road curved left alongside St Mary's church, to avoid boggy ground at the present crossroads, which did not appear until 1896. This 'slough' was drained when the road was built, taking a new course straight up the hill to King's Heath. A small triangle of ground between the old and new roads became the village green – surely the only example of a village with a green of so late a date!

A period of fairly rapid growth began about the middle of the 19th century. Businessmen from Birmingham, three miles away, chose to build their houses on the south side, away from the smoke of the city, which prevailing winds blew away to the north-east; and Edgbaston, Harborne and Moseley became the chosen sites for the large, imposing residences which began to appear around the outskirts of the village. The cutting of the Birmingham to Gloucester railway in 1837 helped to make Moseley popular with industrialists, although King's Heath was the nearest station. Moseley station was not opened until 1867, and closed 'temporarily' in 1940. It has never reopened.

In the second half of the 19th century a wide variety of housing was built, ranging from large mansions such as Highbury (for Joseph Chamberlain), down to the modest terraces, such as Laburnum Grove, which still cluster around the railway line. No factories were built, but many small workshops mushroomed in the backyards of the shops in the village, where small craftsmen were at work. The population rose to 4,000 in 1881 and 11,000 in 1901. A horse-drawn bus service operated from 1859, and steam trams from 1867. These unloved vehicles were replaced by electric trams in 1906. Several fine churches were built, and the parish of Moseley split up between St Mary's, St Anne's, and St Agnes'.

The break-up of the Taylor estates in the 1890s led to the cutting of Salisbury Road in 1896, leading to Edgbaston, and completing the crossroads which is now the village centre. This divided the Moseley Hall Park; the area to the north containing the lake and ice house was bought by a consortium of discerning businessmen who formed the Moseley Park and Pool Co. They built their houses to back onto the Park and fenced it all in. It is now a quiet haven, much appreciated by those who can afford the £17 per annum for a key. A corner of the Park was sold off for the building of a Presbyterian church, and the remainder of the west side of the Alcester Road, previously occupied by the Park fence and gates, was developed with a row of three-storey shops, Victoria Parade.

Edwardian times brought changes in the building scene, and the very large Victorian houses began to give place to more modest houses of high quality, which could be run without a large staff of servants. Many of these were built in the St Agnes and Billesley

Lane area. Amesbury Road and St Agnes Road, which developed at this time, have individual houses designed by some of the most eminent architects of the day, built mainly in the Arts and Crafts manner, a style which was particularly popular in Moseley.

No great physical changes occurred betwen the wars, and this period is looked back on by older residents as a golden age, when the pace of life was slower, there were elegant shops and cafés, literary and dramatic societies proliferated, and everywhere was clean and tidy.

Moseley had its share of bombing, and a serious decline set in after the Second World War; wealthy families had moved out of the large houses, never to return. These houses began to decay and were sold cheaply for conversion into flats and bedsitters, absentee landlords took no care of their properties, the social mix began to change. No large-scale demolitions took place, but two rows of small terraced houses were razed to form a much-needed car park, and a Tesco supermarket, with a garish frontage, replaced several small shops.

Some residents realised that drastic measures were needed to halt the decline, and the Moseley Society was formed in 1979 'to protect a unique area of Birmingham'. The Council was pressurised to do something about litter; the public car park – a tarmac area surrounded by rubbish – was taken in hand by the Society and cleaned up, borders formed all round and planted. No public money being available for keeping the car park clean, the Society took over this job with volunteer labour, and the shop forecourts on Victoria Parade were brick paved and provided with planters. 'Improvement' lines, which would have completely spoiled the crossroads, were vigorously opposed. A watch is kept on all proposed developments and undesirable extensions and infill buildings strongly opposed. The centre of Moseley was declared a conservation area in 1984, and the St Agnes conservation area was set up in 1987.

At the same time there arose a demand for the larger houses, many of which have been re-converted to family homes. These spacious houses with good gardens have tempted many people back into Moseley, and we now have a happy mix of academics, musicians, doctors, architects, students and artists and craftspeople living happily in our cosmopolitan community. A number of our shops are noted for their quality and variety.

Netherton

Netherton stands 700 ft above sea level and commands beautiful views as far away as the Malvern Hills on the Herefordshire borders to the Wrekin in Shropshire. It is said that on a clear day the mountains of Wales are visible. It is now a suburb in the south west of Dudley.

Netherton was once the centre of the nail making industry. At one time many thousands of men, women and girls were engaged in the nail industry. The men made horse-shoe nails, Frost nails, large County Clout nails and the heavy nails used in barge building, also the Tenpenny nails used in roofing. The nail-makers used an 'Oliver' which was worked with a foot treadle to forge out the heavy spike-nails made from 3/8−1/2 inch square and round iron rods.

The women and girls made small clout nails, sprigs, Bromsgrove tacks, sacking nails, tip nails and the round and square hob nails used in the boots of the colliers and ironworkers. The nails used in the building of Hampton Court came from Netherton.

The original accounts state:

'Payed to Raynalde Warde of Dudley for 7,350 of Dubbly Tenpenny Nayles at 11s the 1,000'

The life of the nailers was extremely hard. The whole family was involved in the work, even the tiny children were given jobs to do. They worked hard, swore hard and drank hard. There were unlimited public houses and 'Wobble Shops' where low proof beer, three times stronger than present day ale, was twopence a bucket.

The church of St Andrew was built in 1827−1830 by Thomas Lee, and is described by Pevsner as being 'conspicuously on a hill and in the middle of an ample churchyard with trees'.

The Old Swan inn in Netherton has long been renowned for its home-brewed beer, it being one of the last places in England to brew on the premises.

Canals have been very important to the history of Netherton and at Bumble Hole and Windmill End can be seen the meeting place of several branches of canals. A cast iron bridge carries the tow path over each canal. The famous Netherton Tunnel is

111

nearby, having been reopened in 1984. This was the last canal tunnel to be built in this country, and was so large that boatmen had to 'leg' their way through it. Also nearby, though further up the hill, is the remains of Cobbs Engine House, which was used to pump water from the coal mines.

Newton

The casual visitor today might perhaps be forgiven for thinking that Newton is just part of the urban sprawl, yet it is still possible to see evidence of its recent rural past. The hamlet of Newton grew up near the river Tame about four miles from what is now the centre of West Bromwich and alongside Newton Road, which may have been originally part of a Roman cross-country road called Blake Street.

People have been living in the Sandwell valley for thousands of years and within walking distance of Newton was the 12th century Benedictine priory, at present being excavated, in Sandwell.

Newton Road railway station in about 1840

Sandwell Hall, started in 1609 by the Whorewood family and later completed by the Earl of Dartmouth, occupied the site until this century. The area around the hall was farmland and probably the Dartmouth estate provided work for people in the neighbourhood.

The oldest surviving building in Newton is a small artisan's cottage built about 250 years ago. It was once part of a terrace called The Malthouse Cottages. It is a simple building of brick and timber, just two rooms up and two down. Today it is preserved as a museum, since it was the 18th century boyhood home of Bishop Francis Asbury, the man who is said to have been to America what John Wesley was to England. In Francis Asbury's day the group of cottages faced onto a road which led to some malthouses.

The people of Newton at this time either attended Great Barr parish church or All Saints' church. There was no Methodist church, but prayer meetings were held in Francis Asbury's home, and it was not until six years after his mother died that the first Methodist church was built in 1806. This church has long since gone but the Allen Memorial church, built just before the Second World War, now serves the nonconformists in the area.

Fairyfield House, built at about 1789–90, is the second oldest surviving building. Many people today are unaware of its existence since it is hidden by modern houses and flats. It is an attractive late 18th century house and once had its own grounds – the iron railings which marked part of its boundary can still be seen in Red House Park. The house is said to have an Adam fireplace and deep cellars. In its heyday it commanded an uninterrupted view of the countryside, stretching out to the spires of Walsall and Wednesbury parish churches, with the Clent Hills and the Wrekin on the horizon.

Several early 19th century houses still remain in the area, but unfortunately we have lost one of the most interesting, the original Scott Arms. The coaching inn, built about 1800, played an important part in the neighbourhood. Beer was brewed on the premises – the flavour of which was said to be enhanced by the use of the inn's well water. A cattle market was held there and attracted people from a wide area. The local Magistrates Court was held in the inn and interesting insights into the lives of the local community can be found in the records of the courts. For example people were fined for sheep stealing, cattle rustling or adulterating milk, while some local shopkeepers were accused of adding sand to sugar, etc.

Other early 19th century houses are still in use. Barr House on Newton Road, once the home of a doctor who ran a private asylum there, now consists of several apartments. Another house, in Green Lane, is now a public house, much altered inside but retaining its original frontage. The Red House, standing in its own grounds, is perhaps the best remaining example of early Victorian architecture in the area. It was built in 1841 on the site of a Tudor farmhouse. The house is constructed from red bricks from local brickyards, hence its name. It was the home of a Mr Robert Wellbeloved Scott, a Stourbridge industrialist and Liberal MP for Walsall. Later it passed to other owners, and served as a children's convalescent home, until eventually it became the property of West Bromwich Council. In 1929 the council opened the grounds as a public park. Today Newton residents can enjoy the landscaped grounds and see the features once enjoyed by its previous owners. There is an obelisk in the grounds, a memorial to Princess Charlotte, while near the pool is a 'hermits cave' – the subject of much speculation but in fact a purpose-built garden feature popular in Victorian times. Behind the house is Hill Lane, part of an ancient packhorse road which led to the Delves in Walsall.

The 19th century brought changes to Newton. Newton railway station opened in 1837 and the first train left Birmingham at 7 am drawn by an engine called *The Wildfire*, travelling at the then unheard of speed of 35 mph. The Tame Valley Canal opened in 1844 to provide a means to bypass Birmingham. The canal is wider than most and has tow paths on each side. Today it provides a quiet retreat away from noisy traffic. In the near neighbourhood the Hamstead and Jubilee Pits opened in the latter part of the century, but apart from the annual influx of miners to the area on the gala days, Newton remained a quiet farming community until well into this century.

After the First World War the area began to be developed and, interrupted by the Second World War, building went on apace. By the 1950s and 1960s new estates were springing up, yet retaining the old farm names, such as Pear Tree and Gorse Farm, a link with the past. The motorways came in the 1970s, changing Newton and bringing increasing noise and traffic.

However, Newton is fortunately situated on the edge of the Sandwell Valley Country Park and it is still possible to walk, as Francis Asbury once did, across the fields to Sandwell Park Farm. We also have the Royal Society for the Protection of Birds nature reserve on our doorstep. Our past is all around us and, thanks to present day attitudes to conservation, Newton remains a pleasant area in which to live.

Northfield

The first documentary appearance of Northfield is in the Domesday Book of 1086, when 'Nordfeld' was a manor in the extreme north of the county of Worcestershire. The village had been founded about the year AD 700, by Saxon settlers who cleared high land overlooking the fertile valley of the river Rea. Certainly the site was well chosen and the farming community thrived and extended its territory to cover an area four to five miles long and three miles wide so that, by the time of the Norman Conquest, it was somewhat more important than the neighbouring manor of Birmingham. The large ancient parish of Northfield included many districts long since separated from it eg Selly Oak, Bartley Green and Weoley Castle. It was in the area of Weoley that the early lords of the manor, for many years linked with the lordship of Dudley, established their demesne and homestead in a fortified manor house. The ruined remains of this moated manor house were excavated in the 1930s and can now be seen in the area of Weoley Castle.

The manor of Northfield had an uneventful history, no battle was ever fought within its boundaries, no historic event ever happened there, no mighty family ever made it their home. The old village settlement grew around the church of St Laurence (Church Hill) and for over one thousand years had a peaceful and uneventful history, remaining until the late 19th century a farming community. A common field system of farming was practised in Northfield over many centuries, first on the two course and later on the far superior three course, or Trinity, system – winter crop, spring crop and fallow. Remnants of the so called ridge and furrow, produced by working the large common field system, can still be seen in several areas in Northfield. By the 14th century a gradual revolution was taking place and the lord of the manor was ceasing to be the feudal lord and becoming more akin to a landlord. The land of the manor he leased to the yeomen as free tenants and Northfield became divided into very many small farms. In 1851 there were 52 farms in the parish and even as recently as the 1960s there were several farms still working, but none remain today.

The rural character of Northfield underwent a change in the latter part of the 18th century when, in common with many other parishes on the southern edge of the Black Country, it became involved in the handmade nail trade. Nailmaking was carried out as a cottage industry, often with all members of a family involved and although in many cases it was the only source of income, in other instances it supplemented a smallholding of a few acres or casual farm labouring. The tragedy of the nailmakers was the unceasing lifelong toil of these poor folk, whose lives were forever overcast by the shadow of imminent starvation and eviction from cottage and workshop. In 1831 there were 122 nailmakers in Northfield. By 1841 this had fallen to 74, by 1884 only 23 remained and by 1910 handmade nailing had ceased. Many of the nailers' cottages and workshops still remain, in particular in the Northfield conservation area.

The Northfield conservation area encompasses the area of the old village and the area of original Saxon settlement. Buildings that are to be found in the old village, though few, are certainly not without interest and the church of St Laurence is clearly the most ancient of them. A rebuilt Norman door in the late Victorian north aisle dates the earliest structure and the squat western tower, of a type not uncommon in the Midlands, dates from the 13th century. The finest feature of the church building is the 13th century chancel, which is a perfect example of Early English and Early Decorated periods of English architecture. A very old 16th century wooden porch gives access to the church on the south side and from inside the building the stained glass windows, which are the work of Hardman, can be seen at their best. The absence of monuments in the church is explained by the fact that the lords of the manor of Northfield chose the Priory at Dudley and the Abbey of Halesowen as their last resting places.

Opposite the church gate stands the Great Stone Inn, allegedly a late medieval timber-framed hall house enclosed by an 18th century brick facade. The Great Stone itself was a boulder carried by glacier action from North Wales. From time immemorial it had stood next to the inn, on the corner of Church Road and Church Hill, and was only moved to its present position in the early 1950s. The village pound in which the Great Stone now stands is noteworthy as one of only a handful which survive and it must rank as one of the finest examples remaining in the country. It is now the most direct reminder of Northfield's agricultural past.

Next to the church stands the old St Laurence infants school. Built in 1837 and added to in 1860, this is a very interesting example of an early Victorian Church school, which remained in use up to 1973. It has since been adapted to residential use.

Until the 18th century, travel to anywhere in Britain and certainly in the Northfield area, was very difficult due to the absence of a well maintained road system. Around 1730 far reaching improvements came with the introduction of the Turnpike Trust system of roads. Two such turnpike roads, one from Halesowen to Stratford and a second from Birmingham to Bristol, were to cross at a point about half a mile from the old village of Northfield, resulting in a movement of the centre of the village to this junction. Here a coaching inn, The Bell, was built together with a blacksmith's, a corn chandler's, shops, houses, a workhouse and a village gaol. From this time the Bell Crossing has been the hub of Northfield. When Northfield railway station was opened in 1870 it seemed that the commercial centre of Northfield would migrate again, this time to the area near to the railway. However, the coming of the motor car and motor bus at the turn of the century was to lead to further development along the Bristol Road. In 1898 the parishes of King's Norton, Northfield and Beoley were constituted as an Urban District and in 1911 the Urban District Council was dissolved and Northfield joined the Municipal Borough of Birmingham.

The urban development of Northfield over the past 50 years has been influenced by the fortunes of the Austin car factory located at nearby Longbridge. The demand for a growing workforce prompted several large municipal and private building schemes in the 1920s and 1930s, and further extensive developments in the 1950s

117

to 1970s finally swamped the green-field character of Northfield, which many of the older residents recall with affection. After existing for 1,200 years as a peaceful rural community, the past 50 years has seen Northfield absorbed into the urban sprawl of the City of Birmingham. Newcomers call it Northfield town, no longer village, the old Bristol Road is the High Street and we are no longer served in the corner shop but serve ourselves in the new shopping precinct – this is progress.

Olton 🦋

Olton lies just south of the Birmingham border. It sprang to fame in the 1970s as the place in which Edith Holden compiled her *Country Diary of an Edwardian Lady* which, following publication in 1977, quickly became a worldwide bestseller.

Edith Holden lived in Kineton Green Road, which she refers to as Kineton Lane in the diary. The name Kineton is mentioned in the Domesday Book, the two manors of Olton at that time being Ulverlei and Cintone, from which Kineton was derived.

Hobs Moat formed part of the area known as Ulverlei. Hobs Moat has also been mentioned as being 'Hoggs Moat' and it is thought that it consisted, at one time, of a moat within which was an acre of land upon which possibly a manor or castle was erected – a road nearby is still known as Castle Lane. (The moat is still clearly visible and has been a playground attraction). There were also three large pools which later became meadow land.

Little was recorded of the land for many years but it is known that there were several farms, eg Chapel Fields, Dovehouse, still names of roads in the area. There is a picture of Gate Farm, which used to be on the other side of the Rover works, hanging in the Solihull Council Suite. One of the cottages belonged to two Miss Tromans who were the first siamese twins in Solihull. They had been joined at the neck and, as they were badly scarred because of the separation, they wore scarves and black bowlers.

In 1937 the President of the Ideal Benefit Society presented gifts of land to Warwickshire County Council and Solihull Urban District Council, the most significant being Hobs Moat. This was conveyed under the Ancient Monuments Act 1930/31 and the deeds are still in the possession of Solihull Council. Little was done to preserve the area, but in 1985 a Manpower Services Commission project was established to make an archaeological investigation. Work is still being carried out and earthworks and pieces of pottery, dating back to the 13th century, have been found.

In the 13th century four new settlements emerged, and of these 'Oulton' became the most important. Sir William Odingsel and his wife jointly held the manor of Oulton. The descent of Olton manor from Sir William to the Palmer family is given by *Antiquities of Warwickshire*. The Palmers lived in Olton Hall and were a very charitable family – Henry gave 20 shillings 'mill money' for poor widows and Thomas gave Berry Fields, amongst other property, to provide boys with clothing. Olton Hall then passed to Benjamin Palmer and there is a bust of him in Solihull church.

In 1924 everything was taken out of one room in Olton Hall, including the panelling, and an exact replica of the room was built at the Wembley Exhibition, opened by King George V. Olton Hall was rebuilt in the 19th century and still stands on Lode Lane, but it is now a restaurant called the 'Baltimore'.

Olton Hall and Elmdon Hall were both owned by the same person and in order to maintain Elmdon Hall and the church, furniture was made out of the yew trees. One area of trees was not cut down because there is a cat's graveyard in the grounds and the housekeeper looked after it and insisted that it was protected by the trees – it is still there today. The children from the village school made a colourful sight in their red cloaks and hats going to Sunday school. A tapestry of The Last Supper, done by one of the housekeepers, is hanging in Elmdon church. The Hall was sold to Solihull Council and eventually demolished but the footings are still there.

Olton was very rural until well into the 19th century, and consisted of heaths, woods, farms and cottages, with the occasional Hall or large house. The Warwick turnpike road was built in 1725 and took the route along what is now Ulverley Green Road and Ulverley Crescent.

In 1799 the Grand Union Canal was opened and at the same time Olton reservoir was constructed, to supply water, in times of drought, for the canal. The reservoir is now known as 'Olton

Mere' and the visitor to the area can obtain a good view of this when travelling by train between Olton and Solihull.

It was the coming of the railway that really brought about the urban development of Olton, after the station was opened in 1864. Speculators had been buying up land in anticipation of this, both north and south of the Warwick Road. By the late 1860s most of the land to the south was owned by William Williams, an ironmaster from Handsworth. A covenant was put on his land stating that all dwellings built on the land must have a minimum value of £500. At that time this was a considerable amount of money, which ensured that only those of a certain income level would be able to live on the 'Olton Estate'.

The land was divided into plots when William Williams died, and sold for housing development at a sale which took place at the Hen and Chickens public house in Birmingham in 1869. One of the first buildings to be erected was 'St Bernard's Monastery', now known as The Friary. Its founder was Bishop Bernard Ullathorne and the building was used for the training of priests when it opened in 1873.

The development of St Bernards Road followed, with high class dwellings which were thought to be very desirable by the nouveau riche middle classes of Victorian days. A walk along St Bernards Road is well worthwhile for the visitor to the area today, as most of the Victorian development is still intact, and the variety of domestic stained glass window designs is quite remarkable.

Meanwhile, north of the Warwick Road, the Josiah Mason Trust had bought up much of the land in anticipation of the coming of the railway. In 1873 James Kent, a wealthy business-man, leased from the Josiah Mason Trust 'The Chapel Field Estate', which included a 16th century farmhouse, known as Chapel Fields Farm and a little more than 96 acres of land.

The Josiah Mason Trust largely dictated the type of housing that James Kent was to build. Rows of dwellings gradually ap-peared along Richmond Road, destined to be homes for workers in the lower income bracket. In the early 20th century weekly rents on these houses amounted to 7s 6d, with annual rates of £5.

Larger homes, with higher rents, were built along Lyndon Road and on the Warwick Road leading down into the Hollow. To serve the needs of the now expanding community, James Kent built a row of shops on the Warwick Road in Olton Hollow which he called, somewhat egotistically, 'Kentish New Town'.

He was also a considerable benefactor when a new parish church was planned for Olton around this time and released some of his land for the purpose. Olton was in the parish of Bickenhill until the early 1880s, when St Margaret's church was built. The first vicar was Dr Arthur Butler, who had been curate of St Mary's church, Acocks Green.

The Congregationalists also acquired a chapel at about the same time, on the Warwick Road, situated beside the railway bridge. The building had originally housed both a butcher's shop and a smithy. A purpose built church was later built in Kineton Green Road at the turn of the century. Children from the area could be educated at St Margaret's school (in Richmond Road) which opened in 1885. The Congregational chapel also housed a school until 1893 when the 34 pupils were transferred to St Margaret's school, due to problems with the building. In the early 20th century the Sisters of Our Lady of Compassion opened a convent school at Olton Court.

There were also numerous private schools in the area, though probably the one of the highest repute was Olton College for Girls, which also took preparatory boys. It was housed at Bickenhill Hall and opened for pupils in 1899. Termly fees for younger children were three guineas, increasing to four guineas for girls over twelve years of age.

Thus by the late 19th century Olton had a considerable community, but the setting was still rural and beautiful. There were many farms and farmhouses in the area, including Dovehouse Farm, built in about 1500, in Dovehouse Lane. This is now Olton's only listed building. Chapel Fields Farmhouse was, unfortunately, demolished in 1952.

Edith Holden is not Olton's only famous personage, for Dr Lanchester of motor car fame lived in St Bernard's Road, as did husband and wife team Georgie and Arthur Gaskin, whose influence was very evident in the Birmingham Arts and Crafts movement.

In the meadows which once surrounded Olton Hall and Elmdon Hall now lies the vast complex of Land Rover Limited. Originally known in 1939 as Rover Shadow Factory No 2, it has progressed from wartime aircraft engine production, to its present day position of world leaders in the manufacture of four wheel drive vehicles, Land Rovers and Range Rovers.

Whilst all this technology and engineering forged ahead, Hobs Moat quietly slumbered away until, one cold and windy day, the ancient monument echoed to the strangest whining noise as the world's first gas turbine powered car thundered by, another achievement for the Rover Company. A brief but exciting career developed, culminating in a Rover BRM gas turbine car racing at Le Mans in 1963. The original JET 1 is now honourably retired in the Kensington Science Museum, London. Hobs Moat has long since returned to its old tranquillity, despite the trowels and shovels endeavouring to reveal its long lost secrets.

Olton is now suburban, but community spirit still runs high, encouraged, of course, by the WI which was founded in March 1977.

Packwood 🦢

The earliest record of Packwood is in a deed dated 1190 witnessed by Walter, chaplain of Packwood, and is evidence that there was a priest and no doubt a church. The present church of St Giles dates from the latter part of the 13th century (1270–80) and stands secluded and peaceful in fields, with Church Farm and Packwood Hall as its nearest neighbours. It was at St Giles' church on a June morning in 1706 that a Lichfield bookseller, Michael Johnson, came to marry Sara Ford. Their son, born in 1709, grew up to become Dr Samuel Johnson of literary fame. The registers actually date back to 1668 and are kept in the church safe.

The little church has many treasures, notably the Doom paintings above the chancel arch, dating from the 14th century and rediscovered during restoration work in 1927. There is also an ancient parish chest, dug out from a solid tree trunk and fastened by three locks, the keys of which were held by the two churchwardens and the priest. It is thought that the chest dates from Norman times and would have been used to store church valuables. There is also a fine 18th century chapel, erected by the Fetherston family and containing many of the family's memorial tablets and the family vault.

Packwood Hall, next to the church, is surrounded by a moat and is the manor house of the parish. It stands on the site of a 13th century monastery and has a wealth of timbered work. It is now privately owned. Another nearby property was Packwood Hough, once the dower house of the Fetherston family. This opened as a preparatory school in 1896 and one of its famous pupils was the late Sir Anthony Eden. Packwood Hough later housed education-ally sub-normal boys and was then owned by Warwickshire County Council, by whom it was sold for development. It has been converted into luxury flats, with a small housing estate in the grounds.

About a mile from the church is Packwood House, of Tudor origin, and the home of the Fetherstons from 1598 until 1869. It was subsequently bought by Mr Alfred Ash, who carried out much restoration work from 1905. His son Mr G. Baron Ash, gave the whole estate, with adequate funding, to the National Trust in 1941 in memory of his parents. The yew garden of Packwood House is almost more famous than the house itself and was established by John Fetherston in the 1660s. It symbolises the Sermon on the Mount, with the smaller yews to signify the multitude. On a raised walk, twelve greater yews represent the Apostles while above them four larger ones are known as the Evangelists and on a conical peak above looms the Master. The house has many interesting treasures including some Jacobean panelling and Flemish tapestries.

Packwood is not a compact village, but a rural area straggling around farms and fields with private houses interspersed. It has Darley Mill, with one of the largest millponds in the county. The mill, of 17th century origin, was in regular production until 1933 when the Chamberlain family lived and worked there. Millpool Lane runs alongside and so far has escaped development, so has only three houses in it. Nearby Packwood Towers (1889) had a windmill, from which grain would be sent to Darley Mill when the winds were insufficient to turn its sails.

There was a Free school established about 1845 for the local children, who would walk across fields to reach it (and would pay 1d a week). It was a Church of England foundation and was used also as a community hall for lectures and as a reading room to encourage illiterate adults to become lettered. The last school was built in 1861/62 by Philip Wykeham-Martin MP, who provided the land and the money for the building and the schoolteacher's house attached. Only in fairly recent years has this little place of learning been sold off by the Education Authority, so that Packwood children now attend schools in either Lapworth or Dorridge.

The area known as Packwood today still retains its rural aspect, having several productive farms and many public footpaths, and hopefully will continue to do so.

Park Hall 🌿

Dorothy Windlow Pattison, better known as Sister Dora, ran the general hospital in the late 19th century. Born in Yorkshire, her pioneering work in the field of nursing is legendary. She died on Christmas Eve 1878 and a marble statue was erected in her memory eight years later which still stands today. It is notable because it was the first statue in Great Britain to be erected as a memorial to a woman not of Royal birth.

Pelsall 🌿

Three miles north-east of Walsall, Pelsall has a well documented history. First mentioned in a charter of AD 994, it was part of the estate of Wulfrun, a Mercian noblewoman. At that time the place was named Peolshal, meaning 'land between two streams'. The Domesday entry of 1086 describes it as waste, with only half a hide of land still belonging to the Church. The area had probably been devastated in 1069 by the King's army when dealing with the uprising following the Norman Conquest.

The part of the village known as 'Old Town' was probably the site of the first settlement, gradually becoming more populated, as there was a church in 1311. Records show that in 1332 there were eleven men with movable property of ten shillings or more. In 1801 the population was 477.

Coal was mined in the area and a canal was constructed through the northern end of the village in 1794. Workers and their families were hired and streets were developed. The ironworks were built in 1832 next to the canal and the population in 1851 had grown to 1,132. Due to flooding in the mines and decline in orders at the ironworks, the two industries were closed down during 1890 and 1892. Many lives were lost in the mines and an outbreak of typhoid fever in 1885 and scarlet fever in 1886 caused much hardship, with medical officers urging the laying of sewers.

The most attractive feature of Pelsall is its common, which covers about 200 acres. Over the years it has been controlled by several authorities and improvements have been made with the planting of hundreds of trees. Now it is the responsibility of Walsall Parks Department, who send men out with mowers regularly. In years gone by the grass was kept short by farmers who brought their stock to graze, but the bye-laws now forbid this, also the hanging out of washing which was a common practice of the cottagers who lived on the edge of the grassland.

Over the generations there have been many families whose descendants still live here and it can be confusing to newcomers when married women are still referred to by their maiden names. Many families are related to each other. Until the First World War anyone venturing more than a few miles away was regarded as being very adventurous. There have been many local characters who had nicknames. There was 'Wicked Ant', 'Bloodike' and 'Pigsty Dick' (pronounced Pigstee). 'Wicked Weaver' was the road sweeper. He would carefully sweep up a pile of leaves and turn to get his cart nearer, only to find that a gust of wind across the common had scattered the results of his labour. Then he would jump up and down flailing his arms and swearing to the heavens above. Children walking to the junior school always looked out for him to tease him by dropping a bit of paper, then listen for the yells and screams. Luckily the children could run faster than he could, but were always warned by the grown-ups never to repeat any words he had uttered!

Before the village was declared a conservation area many old cottages were razed to the ground, which had housed large families. It was not unusual for there to be parents and six or seven children in two bedrooms and to eke out the income, a lodger who was a night shift miner (sometimes two) would become part of the family.

Pelsall has for over 100 years been noted for its musical talent.

At least two members of each family would be able to play a musical instrument and/or sing. The village had a silver band, 'The Beer and 'Baccy Band', and orchestras to accompany special events such as Sunday school anniversaries. The latter were invited to the chapels in surrounding villages and even travelled as far as Tamworth in a wagonette. The harmonium was a treasured piece of furniture. Weekly concerts were held in the Institute Hall, part of the Wesleyan chapel property, where there would be a varied programme of monologues, sketches, solos, duets, etc, involving all the village talent. Due to the blackout during the Second World War and the restriction of numbers in a public place, the concerts became less frequent and finally died out.

Today there are many and varied activities for all ages and abilities, some run by the churches and others held in the community centre, which was opened in 1965. Pelsall Civic Society is an active group which acts effectively as the eyes and ears of the village, especially regarding building planning applications. It includes a History Group, who put on an exhibition each year of documents, photographs etc. More than one family has discovered relatives they did not know existed!

Pelsall cannot claim to have produced a national celebrity, but several benefactors have been remembered in street names and the 'natives' recall with affection the three bakers who were in competition early this century. One of them caused a great flurry one day because he forgot to put salt in the bread! The graves of the bakers are side by side in the cemetery.

Pensnett

Pensnett is now a suburb of Dudley, some two miles to the south-west of the town centre. Pensnett is derived from 'pen' – a piece of woodland, or chase, on a hill; therefore, 'the wood on Pen Hill'.

The area around Pensnett had an abundant supply of natural mineral resources, most of which were near the surface and easily worked. It was an ideal region for iron working. It developed rather late compared with some other parts of the country, mainly due to the fact that it had no water power and very little charcoal. It was not until after Abraham Darby's coke smelting process and

James Watt's improved steam engine became available that this area of the Black Country could really use its natural resources.

Pensnett railway opened in 1829 and served the Round Oak Iron Works. The steam locomotive the *Agenoria* was, for many years, the only engine in service on the Pensnett line. The *Agenoria*, now in the York Railway Museum, was named after the goddess of courage and industry. This rail link served for many years to assist the growth of industry in the West Midlands.

St Mark's church in the High Street was built in the 1840s by J. M. Derick. It cost some £6,700 to build and is a typically Victorian church. The south-west spire was not completed, but overall the church is lofty and spacious in design.

Russells Hall Hospital, also in the High Street, is Dudley's new District General Hospital.

Perry Beeches

Perry Beeches is situated about seven miles north of Birmingham city centre and is mostly residential. Not much is written about the history of Perry Beeches because it developed from agricultural land belonging to Perry Hall estate. It is known that Brooklyn College was built on the site of Brookland Farm.

In the 1920s there was some housing development at the top end of the estate but it was not until the following decade, after Perry Barr was absorbed into Birmingham, that extensive building construction began. The Perry Hall estate had been sold in 1928 and in 1934 the land was acquired by the City Council. The First National Housing Trust began building houses shortly afterwards and although the Second World War slowed down the building programme, it was not long before most traces of the area's rural past had vanished.

The parish church of Perry Beeches is St Matthew's. Services were previously held in what is now the church hall, which was built in 1938. The new church was completed in 1964.

The last major upheaval to affect the area was the building of the M6 viaduct through the heart of the estate in 1971.

Quinton 🦢

Quinton lies to the south-west of Birmingham and was once a village clustered around a church. In 1855, the population was around 2,000 people. There was an old toll house, a college (Bourne College) for the sons of Methodist clergymen and a Methodist church. During the 1920s and 1930s the building of new housing estates covered the farmlands of World's End Farm, Welsh House Farm, Four Dwellings Farm and Goodrest Farm. But prior to this it had historical links with Charles II, after he escaped from the Battle of Worcester in 1651. He was thought to have been hidden at Goodrest Farm, near Clent and also at Howley Grange, near Spies Lane. A pike was found in the walls of the latter when it was pulled down.

The name, Quinton, was thought by some to have derived from the meeting of five ways, or the quintain, a device to be seen on village greens, used for tilting practise. However, the Anglo-Saxon Cwenington, meaning 'the queen's town' or 'the woman's town' would seem more likely. The older name for one area is Ridgacre, or 'the ploughed land on the ridge'.

The land for the church was given by Lord Cobham, in 1841. Lord Cobham also endowed the benefice. The church is built of the local red sandstone in the Early English style, has a single bell and several stained glass windows of the Victorian era. The Church school was built behind it and the old churchyard is there too. The old Methodist church, in College Road, was pulled down and replaced in 1976 by a new, purpose-built church. A link with John Wesley goes back to 1781, when he preached in Quinton in a building by Foley's Farm, where the King's Highway now stands.

The old Danilo Cinema, built in the 1930s, was built on the site of a house of a local worthy, called Edwin Danks. It was then called The Classic and now the Cannon chain has converted it to four screens. The oldest house in Quinton lies at the end of the High Street. Called The Nailer's Cottage, it is evocative of the old cottage industry of making nails. It contains the windows of the old toll house, pulled down in 1946. The toll house was situated opposite the King's Highway and was used during the Second World War as a post office. There is a print in the Birmingham Art

Gallery by W. J. Pringle of a stage coach passing Quinton Gate in 1842.

Down Spies Lane, the old road to Worcester, lies a lovely open space, called The Leasowes, which was the estate of the poet, William Shenstone. Another literary link is the fact that the novelist Francis Brett Young lived in nearby Halesowen, where his father was a doctor.

In the Gazeteer of 1855, the village school had 90 pupils, and the headmaster's name was Mr J. H. Huxley. Apparently Mrs Huxley taught the little ones. Quinton was quite a thirsty place in 1855. Names of inns include The Holly Bush, The Red Lion, The Reindeer and The Waggon and Horses in Long Lane. Shopkeepers included victuallers, a butcher, a tailor, a blacksmith and various farmers. Four Dwellings Farm is remembered in the school of that name.

Nailers plied their trade as a cottage industry and a Mr Samuel Dingley, the nail factor, would deliver the raw goods and then collect the finished article and pay out the few pence earned. Apart from farming, that seemed to be how the old Quintonians kept body and soul together. But they seemed to live to a ripe old age, as the headstones in the churchyard bear witness. It is quite a high area, so was probably healthy. The snow seems to lie, long after it has disappeared from nearby Harborne and Edgbaston.

In Kent Road is a sports centre and we are very fortunate to have a large library and leisure centre at Quinbourne, the site of the old Harborne Golf Club's club house. Opposite to this is The Punch Bowl Inn, which was the name of the 17th hole! It is a thriving community centre, fully used during the day and in the evenings.

At the neighbouring village of Bearwood, in Lightwood's Park, is a Shakespeare Garden, containing flowers, plants and herbs mentioned in his plays. Lightwood's House, opposite the old Beeches estate, was the residence of Francis Galton and now houses a stained glass studio of world-wide renown.

In spite of the public campaign to save Quinton Hall, when it was being used as an old people's home, it was pulled down and yet another housing estate built on its site. They have incorporated some of the old names, such as Hoosen Close, Bourne Close and Chantry Drive, to commemorate the old principal and college.

Quinton is now a populous place, a far cry from the little village it once was, but near to the Worcestershire countryside. Whilst we have lost a lot of green meadows, a very nice country park has been landscaped and is a green lung amidst all the new dwellings.

Sedgley ✤

Sedgley is an ancient parish, although now it has been absorbed into the Metropolitan Borough of Dudley. It is about three miles to the north west of Dudley itself. The name is most likely to come from sedge and ley – a sedgy field. In 1272 the inhabitants of Sedgley sold rushes to cover floors of the mansions of the manor.

Although Sedgley stands on a limestone ridge, a sub-surface of clay means that the ground holds water like a sponge.

As far back as the reign of Edward I there is mention of four coal pits and their value is given as £4. The coal that was mined at that time must have been of marketable quality.

The church of All Saints was built in the 1820s by Thomas Lee, under the patronage of the first Earl of Dudley, who paid £10,784. Some memorials from the earlier church have been preserved. The interior is impressive and well worth seeing. Interestingly, there is also a very early Roman Catholic church in Sedgley, built in 1823. It is remarkably grand for so small a place, but is explained by the fact that Sedgley Park was used as a Roman Catholic college for many years. Sedgley Park was once a seat of the Dudley family.

On the edge of the Black Country, Sedgley has had collieries, brick and fireclay works and engineering works within its boundaries.

Selly Oak ✤

Selly Oak is on the Bristol Road, the A38, between Edgbaston and Northfield, and is bordered by Harborne and Moseley. It has within its boundaries Selly Oak Hospital, the Selly Oak Theological Colleges and, though strictly in Bournbrook, part of the University of Birmingham.

Many residents believe that the origin of the name Selly Oak was attributed to one Sarah who was hanged for witchcraft and the stake which was driven through her heart grew into a large oak, hence 'Sally's Oak'.

The name could be derived from Sele-leah, a clearing with a house or hall. Another possible origin, because of the Roman influence, is from salt; the Saltway across the meadow.

The Selly Manor House, which stood on Selly Hill in the line of Icknield Street, was a sub-manor of Weoley. Weoley Castle is now a small district bordering Selly Oak and Harborne; there was a castle or camp there but without a keep. It is said, though not authenticated, that Richard III slept at Selly Manor on his way to the Battle of Bosworth.

Selly remained a hamlet until about 1850 and in 1861 there were 341 houses and a population of 1,483. In the early 1900s, Selly Oak was a peaceful, tree-lined village with cottages, shops, marble horse-trough and a local inn, the Oak, whose licensee was 'Hawk-eye' Lilley, the famous Warwickshire and England wicket-keeper. At that time, 330 acres were taken into care by the Bournville Village Trust. George Cadbury bought the old manor in 1907 and it was reconstructed in Sycamore Road, Bournville.

Selly Oak was well served by both rail and water. The Barnt Green and Cheltenham Railway became part of the Midland Railway. Much of the raw material needed for the emerging heavy industries was carried by the canals. They caused disruption at first as water was drawn from brooks in the Clent and Lickey Hills which also powered mills at Harborne, Bournbrook, Spurries and Pebble Mill. So the two canal companies concerned, the Stourbridge and the Dudley–Worcester, built a reservoir to feed the brooks.

Selly Oak is situated at the junction of the Netherton and Worcester canals and lime was brought by canal and burnt at Sturges' chemical works, (the 'Soap Factory',) manufacturers of citric acid. Another manufacturer was Elliott's Metal Company which brought to the area men skilled in the copper industry. Other firms grew: Hudson's Steel Tubes went on to make Hudson's bikes and Selly Oak was the home of the Ariel motor-bike.

Cadbury's, of course, made a tremendous impact on the area. Apart from building Bournville, their munificence made it possible for various religious groups to start the Selly Oak Theological Colleges, known country-wide and overseas.

The Cadburys themselves were Quakers. Also, John Middlemore founded the Middlemore Emigration Homes in 1872 for settling Birmingham children overseas: 6,729 were received into the homes and 5,412 emigrated to Canada or Australia – unthinkable today!

In 1924, the tram service was extended to the Lickey Hills through Longbridge along the Bristol Road. Part of the excitement of the outing to the Lickeys was the ride on the top deck of a tram: the early ones were open front and rear. Incidentally, there were deep wells at Longbridge and Selly Oak which provided Birmingham with its water until the Elan Valley scheme.

Selly Oak Hospital in Raddlebarn Road was originally the King's Norton Union Workhouse and cost £20,000 in 1872. Those buildings comprise the present School of Nursing. Land adjoining was purchased and a new infirmary opened in 1897. By 1907, more expansion was necessary and by the mid-1930s specialist laboratories and departments grew into the present extensive hospital complex. The famous Queen Elizabeth Hospital was opened in 1938. It houses the University Medical School and forms part of the now considerable university complex.

Selly Oak village is a shopping centre with a large supermarket where the cinema used to be; beyond the railway bridge near the station is the library. The road between Selly Oak and Northfield, the other side of the village, is now a wide, tree-lined boulevard with the Selly Oak Colleges on either side.

Great anguish was aroused locally by the widening of Oak Tree Lane, which caused the great oak first to be lopped back, then moved to Selly Oak Park.

Sheldon

Present day Sheldon, with its vastly increased population, is a mixture of the old and the new. Church Road has been widened past the church; the old bier house, with its bier still intact, was taken down and rebuilt in the paddock behind the modern-day church hall. A reminder of the Second World War, the RAF

Association's Club Room, is housed nearby; and in 1973 the present Women's Institute planted a maple tree, beneath which a bottle, containing several items of interest concerning Sheldon, was buried for future generations.

The old Elmdon Airport, some two miles away, is now a container base. The extended, and much used, new Birmingham International Airport was opened on 30th May 1984 by Her Majesty the Queen. It is connected by 'Maglev' to Birmingham International railway station.

An even more up-to-date innovation is Sheldon Country Park, some 260 acres of open space, which incorporates former farms, playing fields, golf courses and river walkways. Many footpaths remain unsurfaced, thus retaining the former countryside character of the area, and activities for all leisure-minded people are planned. A Head Ranger supervises the park, which is being supported by the Countryside Commission and several other organisations.

How different was the Sheldon of the past. Dating back to at least the 12th century, Sheldon was a parish and scattered village with a mainly farming community. From the reign of Henry I until Edward III, the manor was principally held by a family in the name of Sheldon, being passed down through families until the Grey family sold it to Sir George Digby, whose name is evident to the present day. The Tudor-style manor house, Sheldon Hall, still exists in what was the extreme north-east of the parish.

The name Sheldon derives from the Old English 'scylf dun', meaning an escarpment on a hill, and accordingly, several windmills were built in the area.

The hub of the parish, the church of St Giles, was built in the 13th century, the tower being added in 1461. It incorporates four bells, Santa Maria is 16th century and another is dated 1650, while the smallest was recast in 1723. Of the many windows of the church, 'The Children's Window' situated on the south side of the nave, was so dedicated in 1867, being provided by the children of Sheldon, who raised the money by selling primroses and cowslips in the nearby town of Birmingham. The lychgate was erected in 1899 to commemorate the Rev Jones-Bateman's 50 years as rector – the longest serving rector.

Of the many rectors of Sheldon perhaps the most famous was

Dr Thomas Bray, whose residence Brays House, within Brays Farm, was until earlier this century, surrounded on three sides by a moat. There was a carp pool, providing fish for the table, and trout was available from the nearby Westley Brook. Dr Bray, as the chancel inscription within the church says, 'went out from Sheldon to convey the blessing of the Church abroad'. He formed libraries, established schools and most notably, founded the Societies for promoting Christian Knowledge, and the Propagation of the Gospel in foreign parts (SPCK and SPG).

Records show there were several benefactors of the parish who provided money for 'the provision of cloaks and material' for the parish poor – usually distributed on St Thomas's Day.

Other interesting reminders of history are the two old cottages (opposite the lych-gate) now occupied by the curate; the old school adjacent to the church, established as a charity school by Dr Bray and now a listed building, still used by various organisations; and the old forge (now a timber yard) with the stump of the spreading chestnut tree still intact.

Several inns served the area, including the Bell at Marston Green, the Wheatsheaf, the Wagon and Horses, and the Three Horseshoes, all reminiscent of the farming community. It is recorded that in the 1820s there was much excitement at the Wheatsheaf coaching inn when a large carriage came down the slope from Elmdon and stopped to change horses. A lady sat quietly inside, but a little girl who was with her stood up, swinging her hat. The lady was the Duchess of Kent and the little girl was the Princess, so long to reign over us – Queen Victoria.

Shirley ॐ

Shirley lies eight miles west-south-west of the centre of England, its western and northern limits being the Worcestershire and Warwickshire boundaries. It is approximately seven miles from Birmingham city centre. The earliest traces of habitation in Shirley were found at Berry Mound, an earthwork covering about twelve acres, west of the river Cole.

The name Shirley means either 'a bright clearing' or 'a border clearing' in the Forest of Arden, which was particularly dense hereabouts.

Drawbridge over the canal at Shirley

In 1086 Shirley was a small part of the manor of Ulverley. Before the 19th century Shirley became a convenient resort of Birmingham 'sportsmen' indulging in prize fighting, bull baiting and cock and dog fighting.

In 1829 the Rev Archer Clive became rector of Solihull and took steps to improve conditions in Shirley, a remote corner of his large parish. Up till then the Shirley folk had to walk at least three miles across fields and through rough woods to attend Solihull church. Having obtained a gift of land from his cousin, the Earl of Plymouth (who was lord of the manor), the Rev Clive had a plain chapel built to seat 506 people, at a cost of £1,584. The chapel was built in the Early English style and consisted of a nave and a recess for the choir, with galleries on three sides, looking down on box pews. It had a low square tower at the east end and the altar was placed at the west end. One explanation of this unique arrangement is that noise from the Plume of Feathers inn, on the opposite side of Shirley Street, later to become the Stratford Road, might disturb the worshippers. Shirley St James became a separate parish in 1843, about ten miles by five miles in size, and including Shirley End and Whitlocks End.

The first permanent Baptist chapel was built in 1845, seating 70 people (near the borders of Hall Green) and the present church was built just before the First World War. The present Lady of the Wayside Roman Catholic church and school were built about 1965. In 1927 a disastrous fire destroyed the Methodists' wooden church which had been built in 1890. The present church premises were erected on the same site.

In the early days most of the inhabitants of Shirley were farmers or farm labourers. The Beach family lived at Blackford House for many years (since 1262) and played a leading part in Shirley's affairs. In 1780 Thomas Beach started a small 'weighing instrument' manufacturing business in his outhouse. He moved to Digbeth, Birmingham and was joined by a Mr Avery. The present well known scales business owes its existence to small Shirley beginnings.

There is no concrete evidence that there was a monastic priory on the site of Colebrook Priory, but there are signs of the existence of an earlier building. When a fireplace was being rebuilt, a fragment of a coal bill dated 1789 was discovered. In the garden is a mound ten feet high and 50 feet round the base. A circular path is traced around the smooth round hill and it is supposed that this is a praying mound, dating from the time of a priory being in the area. Colebrook windmill, near Colebrook Priory, was a brick built tower mill, used during the Second World War as an observation post by the police and Royal Observer Corps.

The railway came to Shirley in 1900 and a Mr Warwick who lived at Wood Farm, Bills Lane was largely responsible for it doing so. Shirley station was actually opened in 1908, bringing lots of changes to the area. In the late 18th century and early 19th century the land around the station was mainly used for pig farming. There were also several mills. Shirley Mill was quite a landmark, with its large sails it stood proud on a hill for all to see until the late 1950s or early 1960s, when it was demolished. All that remains now is the mill pond and the ducks and geese.

Green Lane was just a small country lane which ran down to the river Cole and a ford with a little footbridge where the children played. The river Cole was first mentioned as the Colle in AD 849.

It rises near Alcester and flows through pleasant fields until it passes through the industrial heart of Birmingham and finally reaches the Thame. It gave its name to a very famous family and also Colmore Row in Birmingham. Sixty feet above the river on an aqueduct flows the Birmingham and Stratford on Avon Canal. This was the last canal to be completed in the Midlands.

An Act of Parliament was passed in 1793 to build the canal, but the work was delayed and by 1798 it was only navigable as far as Hockley Heath. In 1808 Stratford Corporation advanced a further £2,000 and the work was completed in 1816, linking the canal with the Avon at Stratford.

The canal was used in the early days to bring goods from Birmingham to Stratford and down the Avon to the Severn, and thus to Bristol. But Birmingham Corporation used the canal for bringing barges of household rubbish and there were many tips around the canal. Today this has encouraged many people to come and dig for treasures in the Victorian rubbish.

The canal these days is mainly used for pleasure boats and by fishermen. There is a quaint drawbridge and a nice pub and in the summer people sit and watch the bridge being lifted and the boats passing by, and, of course, also the wild life which abounds around the canal.

Shirley district has grown enormously. Situated as it is on the main A34 which runs from Manchester to Southampton, it is now well served by motorways; the latest M42 junction, only two miles from Shirley centre, links with the M4, M6 and M1, and still to be completed is the Oxford spur M40. Houses have mushroomed, the Cranmore/Widney development alone being the largest in the county with 2,500 houses. It contains also the largest industrial estate of over 100 acres, recently doubled in size and providing over 4,000 jobs.

Shirley has a long history of family ties despite recent growth. There is a successful well-known band, a strong Round Table, active Residents Association, a brand new community centre, opened by the Princess Royal, and the district is well represented by its youth with Boys Brigade, Scouts, Guides, ATC and Army Cadet Force.

Shirley is also proud of its fund-raising activities throughout the world, such as the Our Lady of the Wayside parish who raise millions of pounds for charity. Even the Christmas lights, provided by local traders down the length of the Stratford Road, bring many admiring visitors.

And so the old village of Shirley now almost rates as a New Town, but older residents can still recall when there was a farm there, or a blacksmith on that corner, and where children fed the horses on their way to school. And residents will continue to live either this side or that side of the Stratford Road, which will remain the great divide, despite, as many a motorist will testify, probably having more controlled pedestrian crossings on its two mile stretch through Shirley than anywhere in the country.

Solihull ✤

Solihull is eight miles from Birmingham and 17 from Stratford-upon-Avon. It was founded in the medieval period and there are still many traces of its past today. St Alphege's church, or part of it, dates back to 1270. In medieval times it was a small market town, little bigger than a village, which gradually grew, but by the 16th century the market had declined. The GWR built a station here in 1852 and this attracted manufacturers from Birmingham to take up residence here. In the 1960s great changes took place and Solihull is now the central point of the Borough of Solihull, but fortunately it still retains its beautiful parks, trees and residential homes with well tended gardens. Its library is very extensive

Warwick Road in Solihull

and also contains a 300 seat theatre, exhibition halls and a continuing display of local arts and crafts.

St Alphege's church is dedicated to Alphege, an Archbishop of Canterbury who was martyred at Greenwich in 1012. It contains several chapels and the upper chapel still has its original roof. There used to be three bells, which were increased to six in 1659. These were recast in 1685 and two more added. 1894 saw the further addition of two more and in 1970 the ring was brought to twelve and constitutes one of the finest sets of bells in the country.

About half a mile from St Alphege's church, through Malvern Park, stands Malvern Hall, an 18th century stately home, now a school. Humphrey Greswold was the first builder and when he died in 1712 he was succeeded by his brother, Marshall Greswold, whose daughter Mary married David Lewis. Their son, being known as Henry Greswold Lewis, inherited the property in 1773. He had the main part of the house remodelled, taking his plans from an old design by Inigo Jones, and the entrance hall followed the Adams style.

Constable painted a picture of the Hall on at least three occasions. One of these is in the Tate Gallery, one in a private collection in the USA and the third in France. The artist had been invited to Malvern Hall to paint a portrait of the owner, Henry Greswold Lewis, whose sister, the Countess of Dysart, was a friend and patron of Constable. A copy of this portrait hangs in the entrance hall.

Between 1829 and 1915 the house changed hands many times through marriage and inheritance, but in 1915 it was bought by Horace Brueton, a great benefactor to Solihull. He built for himself a small modern house in part of the grounds and in 1926 Solihull RDC, with Warwickshire Education Committee, purchased Malvern Hall and eleven acres of the land as the nucleus for a High School for girls, and about 16 acres for public access, the latter to be known as Malvern Park. In 1944 Horace Brueton gave most of the land he had retained, including the lake formed by damming the river Blythe, and this now forms Brueton Park.

Solihull is fortunate in having a thriving Society of Arts which caters for all tastes and ages. Founded in 1944, the Society is democratically run by an Executive Committee. There are nine sections:- Art, Antiques, Drama, Records, Film and Video Unit, the Chandos Choir, Opera Section, Local History and a Literary Section which includes a lively discussion circle. As well as regular meetings, there are plays, concerts, interesting visits and excellent visiting speakers.

Solihull hospital developed in what was the 19th century workhouse. 'During my early years in Solihull' writes one resident, 'I well remember my first visit to the local hospital in Lode Lane. I was allocated to a ground floor ward in which the beds were placed either side in an orderly fashion, each bed having a locker at its side. These lockers had no doors, which meant that all your personal possessions were left for all to see. Your dressing gown had to be rolled up and placed in the opening at the bottom of the locker.

'Situated in the centre of the ward was a large, black cast iron stove and this monstrosity provided the heating for the whole ward. Periodically some nurse or orderly had to refuel it with coke, a process which had to be done both night and day and which created a most undesirable cloud of dust and smoke.

'Another feature of the hygiene was the fashion in which the wards were cleaned. Early each morning the cleaning staff would walk round the ward with a large container of used tea leaves, which were thrown indiscriminately all over the floor and under the beds. Inevitably many of these found their way into the open lockers, covering dressing gowns and personal possessions with horrid brown marks.

'If this seems primitive by modern standards it is worth recording, that at this time, part of the hospital also served as a workhouse and many of the menial tasks were performed by the inmates. In fact this continued until the mid 1960s.'

One resident remembers coming to Solihull for the first time in the early 1960s. 'Approaching Solihull via the Warwick Road we were impressed by the large houses at Copt Heath with their beautifully manicured and landscaped gardens. We drove past the distinguished old church opposite the local hotel which had the appearance of an old coaching inn; down the tree-lined High Street bordered by quaint old-fashioned shops. A vivid memory still, is Simpsons on the corner of Station Road, the window display of a wide variety of fish, hares, braces of pheasant in feather and other game hanging by the entrance. This looked like the kind of place we were hoping to spend the rest of our lives.

'We found our permanent home a short time later. A large semi-detached Victorian house on three floors. There was a delightful view over Tudor Grange Park, you did not notice the railway line, and it was very convenient for shops, schools, and walking the children and dogs. The Tennis Club next door was a social attraction, many summer afternoons were spent there until we made our own grass court at the bottom of the garden. The neighbours were friendly, Wrensons in the High Street delivered the groceries (the manager called me 'Madam' when I gave my order), shoes were mended at the cobbler's in Mill Lane in one of a row of beautiful old cottages.

'A quarter of a century later, it has all changed. Solihull is approached by a motorway spur. The church still stands on the hill dominating the town, but the vistas have gone, it is now overwhelmed by the modern council houses and recent extension. The hotel has been enlarged and an out of character modern facade covers the old coach entrance. The High Street remains recognisable by the trees but the shop fronts are modern and plastic, the old grocery is replaced by a sprawling Macdonalds. A Chinese restaurant takes the place of fish and game. The Mill Lane cottages were destroyed with the old police station to make way for a shopping precinct.

'We look at these changes with some regret. It is certainly a new way of life, an old Silhillian can no longer say "I'm just going into the village to do my shopping".'

Stechford 🐿

One resident of Stechford remembers it in the 1920s.

'Stechford in those days was very much a village surrounded by fields, many farms, lovely country lanes and ponds. If one stood at the top of Lyttleton Road, there was an uninterrupted view, over fields, to Yardley parish church and beyond. In other directions, fields and country lanes led to Castle Bromwich, Alum Rock and to Bordesley Green, surrounding the old Yardley Fever Hospital, now the East Birmingham Hospital.

'I was born in Yardley, just over the Stechford border, and Stechford village was always "the village". The first school I attended was in Stechford, held in the Masonic Hall on the corner of Station Road and Manor Road (now a DIY store).

'My grandmother and mother shopped in Stechford, taking me along as a small child, and I can still remember the lovely old shops. First to come to mind, dear old Mr Brittle's shop at the top of Yardley Fields Road, just before the turning to Albert Road. This shop sold almost everything, but it was the barrels of butter which intrigued me most. Then on into Albert Road. On the left hand side was the school (and still is), known in those days as Stechford Council School, built in 1896. Further along was a sweet shop and newsagent's; Holton's the baker's; a ladies out-fitters; Cottrell's the butcher's; Smith's the greengrocer's; Eaves, a delicatessen shop, where as I grew older, my mother would send me for a 1/4 lb of boiled ham, 6d in the old money.

'Next door was a corn merchant's; chemist's; and Oakley's, a good old fashioned family grocer's. Their cheese was a legend. There was always a chair to sit on in the shop, and all orders were delivered. On the other side of the road there was an iron-monger's; outdoor beer licence; a post office with a tinkly bell when you opened the door; Mrs Hen's who sold babies prams, sewing machines, dolls prams, fairy cycles etc, and Bradbury's, who sold everything from a reel of cotton to bed linen.

'On the corner of Lyttleton Road and Albert Road stood a very nice old house with a pretty garden. Here resided the local doctor and his family. He was a very well liked and respected man, who always rode a bicycle. His help could be sought morning, noon and night. I well remember a story my mother told of Dr Gibb, for that was his name. He went off to the First World War a redhead and came back completely white. He was of the Catholic faith and was instrumental in getting Corpus Christi School in Lyttleton Road built in 1934 and was also its main benefactor.

'With the opening of Stechford station, great prosperity came to the area. Many manufacturers from Aston, Hockley and the jewellery quarter, who lived with their families in houses on their factory premises, began moving into Stechford, travelling by train to and from Birmingham. These men were wealthy and took over some of the existing houses in Stechford, others having houses built. Among these manufacturers were Browns, Verneys and Bulpitts, the latter being the makers of the now well known Swan Brand goods. They were great beneficiaries to the village, particularly to the parish church of All Saints, also giving work to many of the locals, as servants, cooks, gardeners etc.

'In 1919 the Parkinson Stove Co (now Thorne Electrics) was built. This proved to be unpopular with many of the residents, who thought the air would be polluted. It was popular with others, as it provided employment for many. Almost at the same time a Railway Laundry was opened in Lower Stechford. This has now gone, houses and maisonettes being built on the site.

'As the years have passed by many changes have taken place. Housing estates have been built and many more shops, and transport has become easier. Trams that ran from Birmingham to Bordesley Green were extended to Stechford. Buses took over some years ago and now run to Chelmsley Wood. The outer circle bus service started in 1926. Two more churches have been built, and we now have a fine swimming baths and community centre. Stechford is now very well populated, a far cry from the turn of the century.

'But I often see in my mind's eye the dear shops of yesteryear and remember the happy times I spent as a child, and in later years, shopping in "the village".'

Stockland Green

The Stockland Green area of Marsh Hill is approximately a mile from the centre of the suburb of Erdington in north-east Birmingham. As its name suggests, it was once a place where cattle were penned.

There have been many changes in the area during the 20th century. The whole area was called the Bleak Hills, and used to have a windmill on its crest. There were many farms at the turn of the century, and Bleak Hill Road and Marsh Hill were just lanes. There were a few terraced houses at Stockland Green and cottages on Marsh Hill.

With the introduction of more modern transport many roads and houses were built.

Tramcars first came to Stockland Green in 1912, the route taking them over three miles from the centre of Birmingham. In 1926 Streetly Road was built, so the tram terminus was moved to Short Heath and continued to serve the population of Stockland Green until 1953. A lot of the older folk of the area look upon the old '78' tram with much affection. Stockland Green has had a bus service from the city since 1953. One thing Stockland Green was famous for was the experimental 'Tracline' that was laid in 1984 to take the buses on a track of 600 yards from Stockland Green down Streetly Road to the terminus at Short Heath. Many lovely mature trees were destroyed to accommodate the 'Tracline', which has now been dismantled. Grass has been relaid but it will be many years before the avenue of trees will reach maturity.

Corporation estate houses were built at Stockland Green and Brookvale in the middle 1920s.

Marsh Hill infants school was built in 1928 to accommodate the young families that had come to live in the area. As the need became greater it changed to an infant and junior school. Up to that time the cornfields on part of the Bleak Hills were still there, but in 1933 the land was sold for building and all the beautiful fields disappeared. Buses had arrived in Birmingham and Marsh Hill was on the Outer Circle bus route. In fact one of the first buses to come down Marsh Hill overturned. It was then felt necessary to make it a compulsory stop because of the gravity of the hill. No longer did people come to the country on Sundays from the inner area of Birmingham to visit Brookvale Park, Witton Lakes, and the country public houses, such as the Stockland and Hare and Hounds on Marsh Hill. They came to live and bring their contributions to life in the area.

Stockland Green had one church, the Wesleyan Methodist, which was started in 1887. The congregation used to meet in a mission hall in Stockland Green until they were able to raise enough funds for a church to be built in Slade Road. The Methodist church, as it is today, celebrated its 100th anniversary in 1987. The mission hall was taken over by St Mark's until its Anglican church was built in Bleak Hill Road in 1928.

Stockland Green was dominated by the Stockland public house, which was built in the early 1920s. This has recently been renovated and thankfully they have kept the old architecture. Many of the older residents will also remember the Plaza cinema with nostalgia, queueing on a Saturday to get in the 'pictures'. Alas it has gone the way of most cinemas; it was turned into a super-market, and now is being turned into a bingo hall.

With the advent of more motor cars Marsh Hill was made into a dual carriageway. The volume of traffic was very great, taking people to their places of work in industrial Witton and Aston.

In the 1960s three secondary schools were built at Stockland Green on land that was once a farm and had then been allotments. One was a bi-lateral school, one a boys technical school and the other a girls grammar technical school. These have now become a secondary school and The Josiah Mason Sixth Form College. Sir Josiah Mason was a notable benefactor of Erdington. In 1987 a modern leisure centre was built on the same campus.

In 1967 Spaghetti Junction was commenced, just a mile away from Stockland Green towards the city. Also the Aston Express-way was opened in 1972, bringing the City of Birmingham even nearer.

Streetly

Streetly is a pleasant residential community, north of Birmingham and adjacent to Sutton Park. Like other established suburban districts it has a great variety of houses in pleasant roads, with a sprinkling of shops and most of the amenities one would expect to find in such a place. What Streetly does not have is a centre, a focal point, and that is because its history seems concerned mainly with roads.

The Romans came, and they built a road about two miles of which is still discernible in Sutton Park. At the time the Romans built their road this area was part of a large forest, but in the Middle Ages the trees were used for charcoal to fire the iron forges in what is now known as the Black Country. The resulting heathland had been developed into farmland by the time the Midland Railway Company built their railroad. In 1879 a station was opened and because of its proximity to the Roman Ryknield Street the station was named Streetly.

The railway ran between Walsall and Birmingham and soon

good class houses were built in the vicinity of the station, no doubt to house early 20th century commuters.

Since that time the farmland has gradually been eroded as more and more houses have been built and Steetly has become a suburb of Birmingham, with farmland only on parts of the north and west sides.

The Chester Road, which runs through Streetly, has been a main route between London and Chester for centuries. Men and horses (and even cars) need regular refreshment, so, on trunk roads there have always been inns at regular intervals. On the Chester Road in Streetly there are three public houses on the sites of old inns.

The 'Royal Oak' became the Parson and Clerk when a legal wrangle between a local squire and a clergyman over the owner-ship of the inn, inspired an artist to paint a sign showing a clergyman kneeling with a lawyer standing over him with an axe.

The Irish Harp is said to have had the name changed at the time of the building of the railway when it was frequented by large numbers of Irish navvies. The Hardwick Arms was previously the 'Five Ways Inn'.

We know something of life at the turn of the century at and around the Hardwick Arms from a lady whose grandmother was the licensee for 29 years.

Mr Henry Jillings was killed in a riding accident soon after taking over the pub. The owner insisted that Mrs Jillings stay on as she was a very capable woman who stood no nonsense from unruly customers.

Mrs Jillings' five children all had chores to do, these included black-leading the grates and cleaning the oil lamps each morning. The children had a long walk to school in Little Aston. The owner of Little Aston Hall, Sir Parker Jervis, allowed the children to take a short cut through his private deer park.

Their disciplined early life must have stood the children in good stead, for the eldest son Alfred, on leaving school at twelve, took charge of the farm next to the inn, he later built the Hardwick Stores and had the first post office in Streetly. The eldest daughter Rachel could have stayed on at school and become a teacher but she was needed to help her mother, so she also left school at twelve. She had a drapery shop in the vicinity for many years. The youngest daughter, Annie, played the piano in the bar when local

146

singers entertained the customers. In those pre-First World War days, the beer was 2d a pint, whisky 2s 9d a bottle and tobacco 2d per ounce – but wages were also low.

At this time in Streetly there was no church, cemetery, doctor or policeman and people were accustomed to walking long distances. Streetly now boasts churches of various denominations, a crematorium as well as a cemetery, and many doctors, though no police station. The public houses have all grown beyond recognition, Little Aston Hall has been converted into apartments and there is a private hospital in the park. Where once a forge stood is a garage and the general stores is now a Chinese restaurant. Where huntsmen in scarlet rode their horses, cars rush at 40 miles per hour across land that was a marsh when the Romans built Ryknield Street. The road names are a reminder of the past, of farms, families and countryside.

Alas, the station that gave its name to the whole district of Streetly no longer exists. It was closed in 1965.

Streetly Blackwood 🦋

The name Blackwood can be seen on 16th century maps and it is thought to have come about because the area was planted with dark pine trees. In the 1920s fire damaged the wood and to some local people the name 'Blackwood' was reinforced because of its black charred appearance.

The old black wood of pine trees was felled to make good timber shortages during the Second World War. Old cottages were demolished and building estates rapidly devoured the green fields to produce the Streetly Blackwood we know today.

Sutton Coldfield 🦋

Lying on the A38 road to Lichfield, and some seven miles north-east of Birmingham, Sutton Coldfield is steeped in history and tradition.

Early records show that it originally consisted of a single main road about a mile in length. Icknield Street, sometimes known as

Ryknield Street, one of the finest examples of the Roman road builders' art, runs from Sutton Park to join the famous Watling Street. About the time of the Domesday Book, the manor of Sutton was in the ownership of William I, and it passed through the hands of several of the English Kings, until the granting of a Royal Charter in 1528 by Henry VIII to Bishop Vesey, Sutton's most famous son. This gave Sutton Coldfield the right to be described as 'Royal', and set out in detail rights and privileges for its administration. Thus the designer of a form of local government for the organisation of a community was none other than the good Bishop himself.

Born John Harman, the son of a local yeoman farmer, he was a brilliant scholar, educated at Magdalen College, Oxford. He assumed the name of Vesey and, finding favour at the court of Henry VIII, where he was tutor to Princess Mary, the King's daughter, was raised to the Bishopric of Exeter in 1519. Through his friendship with the King he was successful in persuading the monarch to grant the Royal Charter. Vesey was a man of foresight and fresh ideas, many of which are still evident today. He set up schemes for the many unemployed – indeed these projects may have been forerunners of the current job creation systems. He set them to work, paving the town, repairing roads and tried, unsuccessfully, to introduce weaving into the town. He built 51 stone cottages, and endowed a grammar school for boys, whose pupils have, to this day, a bishop's mitre as their school badge. He was also instrumental in building two aisles on to the parish church of Holy Trinity, wherein his tomb lies enshrined. However, the most important gift which he made is Sutton Park.

This vast Park has been preserved in its natural state, and the woods, moorland, gorse, heather, streams and pools which form its beauty have given much pleasure to residents and visitors alike over the centuries. In the early days hunting and fishing took place, and the people were able to graze their cattle and sheep. Cattle are still grazed there today. In more modern times the Park played host to the world-wide Scout Jubilee Jamboree, when thousands of Scouts from all over the world were accommodated. More recent events have been the annual carnival, and cars in the Lombard Round Britain Car Rally find part of their route is through the water splash. The Park has recently been designated as a site of

'Special Scientific Interest', and the 'Friends of the Park', a society to which many Suttonians belong, keeps a watchful eye to see that this precious possession is not abused or altered in any way and that it remains in its natural state.

After the death of Bishop Vesey, Sutton Coldfield resumed its rural character as a market for the surrounding area. It remained small, in character more of a large village, with varying fortunes. Charles II granted a new charter in 1662. Some time during the 17th and 18th centuries industry began to develop in the area, due it is believed, to the very good water supply in the neighbourhood. Mills were erected, and a thriving trade began to grow. Cotton spinning formed a part of the industrial life, and one of Sutton's own sons, John Wyatt, invented a piece of mechanical equipment for spinning cotton. However, about this time steam power began to take over from water power for driving the mills. Gradually the cotton and other industries began to decline and finally disappear, and today Sutton is mainly residential.

In 1862 the steam railway came to town, the London and North Western ran between Birmingham and Sutton Coldfield and in 1879 the Midland Railway first ran through the Park. In 1956 the diesel train service between Birmingham and Lichfield, was inaugurated; it ran through Sutton Coldfield and is widely used by local commuters, although the route through the Park is used now for freight only.

Other famous sons include Dr Bodington, who, in the year 1840, is said to have advocated 'The Rational and Scientific treatment of Pulmonary consumption'. Bodington Gardens at the south end of the town are a lasting memorial to this remarkable gentleman.

A flourishing leisure centre, attractive swimming baths and a delightful shopping centre are some of its present day facilities. An excellent library, with numerous departments, and a large busy hospital, aptly named 'Good Hope', are among them. Numerous societies flourish, among them musical and theatrical groups, along with many differing religious persuasions. The roots of its rural, village, past are however still there to be discovered.

St Mary's church and The Old Hall, Temple Balsall

Temple Balsall 🪶

Temple Balsall, a settlement in sylvan, tranquil countryside on the river Blythe, is far removed in spirit froim the hurly-burly of the nearby conurbations. With no shops or pub, it is a place of retreat, and so it has been for over 800 years. Little has changed and yet it has such an outstanding and stirring history.

In the 12th century the manor was given by Roger de Mowbray to the crusading Knights Templars – hence the name. They built a Hall (part of which remains), a chapel and farmed the estate. These soldier monks were suppressed and disbanded in 1314, being succeeded by the Knights Hospitallers – another great crusading Order. It is to the latter that we possibly owe the foundation of the present church. The Knights Hospitallers, in turn, were disbanded by Henry VIII, after which came years of neglect for the settlement. Eventually, the manor came into Crown hands and Queen Elizabeth I gave it to Robert Dudley, Earl of Leicester, it later being inherited by his granddaughters, Lady Anne Holbourne and Lady Katherine Leveson. Lady Anne restored the church and Lady Katherine, by her will in 1674, founded the almshouses for poor women and a school for poor boys. A board of trustees or governors was set up to administer the charity, funded from the revenues of the estate of the old manor, which is still run today by their successors (updated to reflect modern needs).

Turning off the Fen End Road into Bread Walk you will find The Court (The Hospital of the Lady Katherine Leveson). Beyond the beautiful wrought-iron gates is a medieval courtyard – two storey buildings on either side and The Master's House (the vicarage) at the far end. The impression is of mellow bricks, roses and flowering plants. Inside are modern flats, centrally heated, each with bedroom, sitting room, kitchen and bathroom – very different from the accommodation provided for the 'Dames' of old. Today's residents are of both sexes, have a warden and will shortly have full 'care' and nursing facilities available.

In the corner of The Court is the old schoolroom, now known as The Prayer Room and used as a social room. In the Prayer Room is the original schoolmaster's desk and the benches around the walls.

Here also refreshment is provided for today's pilgrims to Temple Balsall on weekend summer afternoons, by the ladies of the parish.

Continuing along Bread Walk we come to St Mary's church, restored in the 1670s by Lady Anne Holbourne, when it became the chapel of the Lady Katherine Leveson Hospital and where the Master and the 'Dames' said prayers twice daily.

In the 1840s Sir Gilbert Scott was commissioned to restore the church yet again and today's building is largely his work. On entering the church one is immediately aware of the great east window. The glass is early 20th century and the central panels depict scenes from the Gospels. The outer and lowest panels show the arms of Lady Anne Holbourne and Lady Katherine Leveson, and others the arms of the Grand Priors of the Order of St John of Jerusalem (the Knights Hospitallers). A distinctive feature of the church is the steps down the nave, which some people think correspond with the grades of service in the Order of the Knights Templars. As the present church was not built by them, this can hardly be so but it is an interesting point. The west (rose) window is of rich colour. Attention must be drawn to the magnificent altar kneeler, 27 ft long, which was worked by over 200 friends of the parish in the mid 1980s. It depicts life at Temple Balsall throughout its history.

Past the church is The Old Hall, the surviving building of the Preceptory of the Knights Templars and the Knights Hospitallers. The building is now encased in fairly modern brick but the massive roof supports of tree trunks can still be seen. Both the upper room and parlour have a wealth of exposed oak. It is in this building that the present-day governors of the charity meet. In the 17th and 18th centuries the bailiffs of the estate lived there and a few years ago a cellar nearby was excavated, revealing an extraordinary hoard of pottery and glass. This valuable collection of 17th and 18th century domestic ware is now in a local museum.

Temple House, opposite to The Old Hall, is now the home of the tenant farmer. This lovely 18th century house was built for the bailiff of those times, following his departure from The Old Hall. Is that why he threw his pots away?

Back along Bread Walk (the 'Dames' used to traverse the path to collect their loaves) we come to the present-day Lady Katherine Leveson junior and infant school. The oldest part was built in the 1850s to replace the boys school held in The Prayer Room; the newest, Wheatley House (named after an ex-Chairman of Governors, the late Mrs Christobel Wheatley, of Berkswell) is a nursery unit. The school is thriving and gives a good primary education.

And so, Temple Balsall looks to an optimistic future, strengthened by its historic past.

Tettenhall ✒

On the edge of Wolverhampton, Tettenhall still manages to retain something of the quality of a village, with its old houses and green.

'Teotta's Halh' (Teotta's Valley) has over the years become Tettenhall. It lies in the part of the Midlands which was freed by King Alfred's son, Edward the Elder, from continuous raids by the Danes. In AD 910 a Danish force was surprised here and overwhelmed in a great battle.

Charles II after his escape from the battle of Worcester in 1651 was hidden in an oak tree at Boscobel. To reach safety he may have made his way through Tettenhall. At Wightwick Manor there is a four-poster bed in which it is claimed that Charles slept. Wightwick Manor itself was built for Theodore Mander in the 1880s, and was given to the National Trust in 1937. It contains many treasures of William Morris and of the pre-Raphaelite painters.

During the Civil War Tettenhall was in 'no man's land' between the King's garrison at Dudley Castle and the Parliamentarians at Stafford. Both sides were able to 'persuade' local people to give money and support to the upkeep of the garrisons. Sir Walter Wrottesley, head of the chief local family at that time, tried to remain neutral, or so he said – but the presence of a Royalist force at Wrottesley in the early part of the war led to him being fined £1,512 10s 0d by the victorious Parliamentary forces later.

The Wrottesley family of Wrottesley Hall (since demolished), played a part in the history of Tettenhall and of England for 800 years. Many of the family were buried in the village church.

On 1st September 1766 James Brindley, the most famous of all the canal engineers, cut the first turf in a field at Compton. Thus began the Staffordshire and Worcester Canal, which was to open up the region to trade and industry. Another means of transport, the development of the mail coach services, increased the importance of the village, as it lies on the main London to Holyhead road. Great improvements came when Thomas Telford, the builder of roads and bridges, was given the task of rebuilding the Holyhead Road.

There has been a church in Tettenhall since the days of King Edgar, a thousand years ago. The tower of the present church is 600 years old, but the rest of the old church was completely destroyed by fire in 1950. Rebuilt within a few years by Bernard Miller, this is an attractive replacement.

Tidbury Green 🍃

Tidbury Green is the smallest of three settlements which for the past 24 years have made up the parish of Hockley Heath.

Originally under the jurisdiction of Solihull, under the 1963 Order when Solihull became a Borough, it was transferred to Stratford-upon-Avon Rural District and combined with Hockley Heath to form the parish of Hockley Heath. The parish also later took in the new village of Cheswick Green, developed on the 'Mount' site a mile or two from both Tidbury Green and Hockley Heath. In the 1974 Local Government reorganisation, when Solihull became a Metropolitan Borough, the parish returned to Solihull but retained its Parish Council and associated limited autonomy.

Tidbury Green is on the western edge of the parish and of the Borough adjoining Wythall parish in Hereford/Worcester county. It seems to have taken its name from Stephen Tyberes, or Tybray, who in the reign of Edward III gave 'a piece of land in "the Market Town of Solyhull, with a building thereon" for the use of the inhabitants of Solyhull.'

The present Tidbury Green dates only from the mid 1920s. Until then it consisted of a number of farms and a handful of private houses, as well, of course, as Fulford Hall, which was built by Colonel Johnstone in 1887/90. Col Johnstone was killed in a fall from his horse on 13th June 1895, and a stone in the verge in Fulford Hall Road marks the spot where it happened.

The old GWR North Warwickshire line from Snow Hill and Moor Street, Birmingham to Stratford forms the western boundary of the parish, with a station at each end of Tidbury Green. The completion of the line just prior to the First World War was no doubt a stimulus to development in post-war years, notably along Tilehouse Lane and Fulford Hall Road about the middle 1920s, and further building took place in the 1930s. There has been little expansion since the Second World War as Green Belt policy has been fairly strictly applied, though some infilling has taken place. Tidbury Green now has some 450 private residences and about ten or a dozen farms. It is about one and a half miles from the M42 motorway, the building of which caused much local anxiety but has proved very beneficial in relieving the village of virtually all heavy goods traffic.

There is a thriving infant/junior school, built in 1931, which was threatened with closure in 1981 when numbers were down to about 70. However, the villagers as one went into battle and persuaded the Education Department to reverse its decision in 1982. Numbers are now up to the 100 mark, and a new brick built school may soon replace the old wooden accommodation.

The centre of the village lacks a church, though there is a Methodist chapel and a mission of Shirley St James, each within a half-mile radius. There is a garage which is also a sweet and paper shop, a farm shop selling fruit and vegetables, and a post office cum grocer's. The village is also without a public house, though there are three about a mile distant. For many years there was a flourishing Village Produce Association which held an annual Flower & Vegetable Show on the school premises. Alas! this no longer exists and although it is missed by many of the older generation, has failed to inspire support among the younger population. There used also to be a Youth Club, Scouts and Guides. However, with the promise of a village hall to be built by the Parish Council in the near future, it is hoped to rekindle the true village feeling once more.

Upper & Lower Gornal

There are numerous suggestions for the derivation of the name Gornal. It could be from the Anglo-Saxon 'cweorn', or from Middle English 'quern', therefore Cweornhale, that is Mill Meadow, or Mill Valley. Some suggest Gor-on-al or 'sun worship'. But it could come from gorn or gwan, a small round tub with handles which was used to carry the wort during the brewing of beer. Beer has been brewed in Gornal for many generations.

This is a typical 19th century industrial landscape, between Sedgley and Dudley. People here are proud of their identity and the local dialect is thought by some to be descended from the Chaucerian English of the Middle Ages. The closure of the local pit in 1968 was a great blow to this close community.

St James' church at Lower Gornal was built between 1815 and 1823, and was enlarged and modernised at points throughout the century. St Peter's in Upper Gornal was built in 1840, and is the plainer and more utilitarian of the two.

In the latter part of the last century, there was much distress and hardship in Upper Gornal. An item from the parish records reads:

'January 1879.
To alleviate the distress in this place, a meeting was convened by the Vicar the Reverend N. A. H. Lewis, and other influential gentlemen in the National Schools when it was proposed to have a soup kitchen. A committee was formed. Mr Jno Peacock offered his premises and undertook to make 100 gallons of soup twice a week which was accepted and has now been done to the great relief of many who appeared truly thankful for it.'

The soup and loaves were distributed at the Jolly Crispin Inn and the Green Dragon.

Walmley

It is difficult to realise that within living memory Walmley was but a small village, with its post office, the Fox Inn and Norman-style blue brick church built in 1842; cottages with walled gardens, interspersed with a few larger houses occupied by the 'gentry', lined the dusty road.

The name Walmley may be derived from the Saxon 'Woam Lea' – the Home Close; and it was at nearby Peddimore Hall, with its double moat and inscription 'Deus noster refugium' (God is our refuge), that William Shakespeare is said to have visited his kinsmen, this being the home of the Arden family. One wonders if he was reminded of those visits when in *King Henry IV*, Falstaff addressing Bardolph says 'Get thee before ... fill me a bottle of sack ... we'll to Sutton Cofil' tonight'.

Penns Hall, with its pool and stream, was first known for its wire mill, the first wire being produced there by Joseph Webster in 1766. One hundred men were employed there in 1813, when there was a great demand for manacles for slaves and malefactors, as well as for piano wire and wire for crinoline dresses. Without its

Walmley

resilience the dresses (so it is written) would have been quite impracticable and the lasses who wore them would have looked like collapsed blancmanges after any public function! As a five star hotel today, it provided the setting for ITV's *Crossroads* motel.

The business was carried on by three generations of the Webster family and the employees of an earlier member spent several years constructing a large lake with spade and barrow. Penns Lake, which is still in existence today, is where during the Second World War, a ten year old girl found an unexploded bomb. With her friends, it was decided to take it to nearby Penns Hall but they were sent away by a maid. As the bomb was getting heavy to carry, it was partly dismantled and taken into Penns Lane. This frightening escapade ended happily for all concerned.

The 1800s brought many changes to Walmley, and a new school was built in Fox Hollies Road which still stands today. It was for 20 girls and 20 boys, for whom clothing was provided, the income for which was derived from the sale of timber. Then in 1851 a girls school was built near the church for 150 pupils; it is interesting to read that infants joining at the age of six should be competent to read monosyllables. That school has now been demolished but some excellent new ones have been built to accommodate the rapidly growing population.

New Hall has had a long and interesting history. A manor house recently converted to a luxury hotel, it dates back to the 12th century and is listed as one of the oldest properties in England. Until recently it was the home of the late Sir Alfred and Lady Owen, so closely associated with BRM (British Racing Motors). It lies in a beautiful pastoral setting, surrounded by a lily-filled moat with drawbridge, and lovely spacious well-kept grounds.

Newhall Mill, still in use today, has been a fascinating place for children for generations. In 1903 Benjamin Styles, the miller, wrote the following poem which tells its own story —

'I'm an old water mill in Walmley near Sutton
I do my work well and I don't care a button
I've stood all my life on this very same spot
I use the Park water, and I don't waste a lot!
I have a good friend in the Squire at the Hall
I supply all the flour as fast as they call.

I ground some wheat once, that was reaped that same day
In less than six hours it was bread on a tray.
There were seventy nice loaves so good to digest
Everyone said 'twas a very good test
The demand for the bread which was very keen
That a loaf was sent to our beloved Queen
In conclusion, I ask you to give me a call
And leave some good order for the mill at New Hall.'

In May 1817, an incident occurred that made legal history. Mary Ashford (a local girl) had been to a dance at Tyburn House nearby with Abraham Thornton, but next morning her body was found in a pit in Penns Lane, and Thornton was accused of her murder. Pleading 'Not guilty' he threw down his gauntlet and demanded 'Trial by Battel'. With no-one to challenge him, he was acquitted, and later this law was repealed.

Mary's tombstone in Sutton Coldfield churchyard reads

As a warning to female virtue
and a humble monument to female chastity
this stone marks the grave of
MARY ASHFORD
aged 20 years

The ghost of Abraham Thornton is said to have been seen walking across the fields in Penns Lane at midnight.

Marching through Sutton Coldfield in 1827, the advance guard of the Duke of Cumberland's army enquired the way from a poor fellow who had no roof to his mouth, but thinking him a spy they executed him there and then. Striking off his head, they carried it on a halbert to New Shipton, tossing it into a tree, having thrown his body into a ditch on the Eachelhurst. A few years later both head and body were found, one at the felling of one of the finest oaks in Walmley, the other at the draining of the meadows (now Pype Hayes Golf Course).

Housing developments began to take place in the 1920s and 1930s and have continued until now, when almost every available space has been filled and the winding country lanes, the hedgerows and fields of wild flowers are no more.

The residential area that has arisen south-east of the village used to be wild poppy fields, which seemed to go on for ever. The new residents probably still find what are now unwanted weeds in their immaculate gardens. The farm that overlooked the poppy fields was where eggs were sold, which were sometimes still warm and village children could visit the new born calves. Cows also grazed in fields off Walmley Road and these were high on the list of visits, when wheeling the pram or push-chair. Now the Canwell Show is the easiest place to encounter real farm animals. Where do mums take their children now? Trains still pass under the railway bridges but only goods trains and if one misses the engine driver, there is no one else to wave to and get a wave in return.

One villager recalls, with much amusement, that earlier this century complaints were made to a local farmer because of the noise created by a very small boy, who was paid one penny a day to shout loudly in order to scare the birds from his cornfields.

Another resident remembers that during the First World War, Mr Forge the local vicar was often seen shovelling coal delivered to the roadside into the coal houses of his elderly parishioners. This same clergyman kept pigs and grew vegetables in the vicarage garden to augment the wartime food shortage in the parish.

Although Walmley has seen many changes, it is still a very friendly place, and one retains many happy memories of days gone by. Walmley is still a caring community. We have many tree-lined roads, a small wood, several churches, five schools, a large medical centre, golf club, two public houses, men's social club, splendid library, an emerald bowling green, a good variety of shops and three Women's Institutes.

Half of our village green was taken away to provide car parking space, but whilst the other half remains, we can still refer to our interesting part of the West Midlands as Walmley Village.

Wednesbury 🎵

The name 'Wotan's Burh' or 'Wotan's fort' places Wednesbury in a very small group of English places whose names show that the original settlers were Anglo Saxon. It is believed by some that there was a temple to the Norse god Woden on the hilltop where St Bartholomew's church now stands. The first settlement has been dated sometime before the middle of the 7th century, although it is thought that it was here that a great battle was fought in AD 592 between Saxons and Britons.

St Bartholomew's is medieval, with a 14th century tower arch and an earlier north aisle. There are a lot of treasures here, one of the most unusual being the medieval lectern. This remarkable creation in wood, plaster and gilt, represents a fighting cock. There is also a 17th century carved oak pulpit which must be one of the best examples in the West Midlands.

Sports of all kinds have always been popular in the area. At one time Wednesbury was the centre for 'cocking' or cock fighting. People came from all over the country to see cock fighting in the cock-pit in Potters Lane. It always took place at the time of the Wednesbury Wake.

As the Industrial Revolution progressed so there grew up in the Black Country a labour force organised on the 'Butty' system. This system was used throughout the collieries, ironworks and in the nailing industry. In the collieries, for example, the proprietor provided the winding machinery and, usually, the labour at the pit-head. Labour underground was engaged by a chartermaster or 'Butty' under contract to the proprietor, who paid him a fixed price per ton of coal. In nailing the work was put out by sub-contractors called 'Foggers'. The product was then sold to the nailmonger with whom there was a contract. This system led to grave abuse, the 'Butties' and 'Foggers' paid the workers in goods through the 'Tommy' shops and in Wednesbury even the masters opened 'Tommy Shops' at the factories.

A great event took place on 14th November 1854 – the opening of the Birmingham, Wolverhampton and Dudley Railway, later part of the GWR. Large crowds watched the first train, drawn by an engine called *Wildfire*. It pulled eight First Class carriages, each with its own name printed on the side. One and a half hours later the second train of Second Class carriages was allowed through. With 'full steam up' an unheard-of speed of 35 miles an hour could be reached!

Two men who had a tremendous influence on the whole area were John and Charles Wesley, the famous preachers. Methodism grew rapidly. There were riots in the town on several occasions and, once, John Wesley's life was threatened. His calmness and quiet demeanor so impressed the crowd that they let him go, and many were converted.

This ancient village has for many centuries been a centre of heavy industry. Wednesbury Forge existed in the days of Elizabeth I, and iron and steel production became important, as did locomotive and other engineering works. Yet even though such industry has brought ever more development to Wednesbury, it still manages to retain a certain character of its own. Perhaps it dates back to those first worshippers of Woden on the hilltop so many centuries ago!

Wednesfield ✤

Wednesfield, just two miles north-east of Wolverhampton, is possibly the oldest of the Black Country townships. It is another place dedicated to Wotan, the Anglo Saxon god, with the addition of 'field' or open land. The name 'Fallings' at Falling Park and Old Fallings indicates woodland felled by the axe and comes direct from the Early English 'feallen'. There was quite possibly a pagan shrine to Woden in the vicinity of Wednesfield.

It was in this area that, in AD 910, Alfred's son Edward defeated the Danes with his Mercians and West Saxons.

At the beginning of the 19th century the artisans of Wednesfield had established the monopoly in the manufacture of animal and man traps. They held this monopoly for one and a half centuries. These traps were for arresting or killing, they were not the cage type. The animal traps were used in the fur trade. Many of the man traps went to the estates of the landed gentry and the plantations of the slave owners. The trap makers were specialised blacksmiths.

The church of St Thomas was built in 1751, but it was burned down in 1902 and rebuilt a year later. Wednesfield reached its time of greatest prosperity in the 19th century, but the skills and trades developed then (with the exception of man traps!) are still supporting it today.

Willenhall ✎

Willenhall was an early Saxon settlement – 'The Meadowland of Willa'. Willenhall was mentioned in the Domesday Book in 1086.

A notable local family are the Levesons. Sir Thomas Leveson was Royal Governor of Dudley Castle during the Civil War. He had been Vice-Admiral of England in the reign of Queen Elizabeth I, and took part in the daring attack on Cadiz. His effigy in Wolverhampton church shows him as one of the heroes of old romance. The present-day representatives of the family are the Leveson-Gowers. The head of the family is the Duke of Sutherland.

Willenhall first began to make keys in Queen Elizabeth I's time. Lock-making became the local speciality, and it was said that the people of the village were hump-backed because of the hours they spent over their work.

In the mid 18th century it was said of Willenhall that it was 'one long street, newly paved' and that 'more locks of all kinds are made here than in any other town of the same size in England and Europe.' There were then nearly 150 lockmakers in Willenhall, and by the mid 1800s the number had increased to over 300. This was a highly skilled trade, and it was only in the 20th century that machinery was extensively used. Willenhall is still a centre for lock making and the iron and brass industries.

In 1966 local government boundary changes brought Willenhall into the borough of Walsall.

Wylde Green ✎

Some interesting stories concerning highwaymen have come out of Wylde Green, now a part of Sutton Coldfield.

The route from Erdington Lane to Coldfield Heath through Wild (Wylde) Green has always been of evil repute. Sir William Dugdale recorded that one Elias-Le-Collier was robbed of £300 on the Ridgeway of Sutton (the old Chester Road) as long ago as Edward I's time, and sued the Hundred of Hemlingford for the money.

On 1st October 1750, the *Birmingham Gazette* reported an incident, also on the Chester Road. On the previous Wednesday, two highwaymen stopped a Mr Henry Hunt and stole his watch and money. However, when Mr Hunt asked the 'knights of the road' to give him back some silver, one returned him six shillings and then rode off to rob another gentleman they had sighted across the Coldfield.

The most notorious highwayman on the Chester Road was Tom King – friend and rival of the immortal Dick Turpin.

On the morning of Tuesday, 27th May, 1817, the body of Mary Ashford – a gardener's daughter from Erdington – was raked out of a marl-pit in Penns Lane, Wylde Green. The marl-pit has long since disappeared and has been replaced by houses and a school in Holifast Road, Wylde Green. The girl was last seen in the company of a young man named Abraham Thornton, a bricklayer who lived in Castle Bromwich. The previous evening, a Whit Monday, she spent her time at the Tyburn House, Erdington, where she danced almost exclusively with Thornton.

Thornton was later arrested and charged with Mary Ashford's murder, but was subsequently acquitted. By this time great public interest had been aroused in the case and local people were quite convinced that Thornton was guilty and had indeed 'brutally violated and murdered Mary Ashford'.

Strangely, further interest was aroused in Mary Ashford's death in 1974, when staggering coincidences were drawn between her and a girl murdered at this time. The girl's name was Barbara Forrest. She had worked at the same place as Mary Ashford had – Pype Hayes Hall; the man alleged to have murdered her was also of the name Thornton and he too was arrested, tried and acquitted, as the evidence was also inconclusive. Barbara Forrest also went to a dance – in the city centre – the night before she died; she, like Mary Ashford, changed clothes at a friend's house, and both girls were of the same age. Further, even stranger, coincidences were also uncovered. Their bodies were found within yards of each other and most unbelievably of all – both deaths occurred on a Whit Monday and on the 27th May. The only real difference was a 157 year gap!

John Harman, who later became Bishop Vesey, was the tutor of Mary Tudor, the daughter of King Henry VIII and Catherine of

Aragon (his first wife), who was later to become Queen. He built many houses in and around Sutton Coldfield for his workers and was well known as a social reformer in the region.

The Vesey Cottage, built by Bishop Vesey in the late 16th century, still stands on the bend of Wylde Green Road. It was built of red sandstone rubble with ashlar angle-dressings and stone mullioned windows, and a doorway which had a triangular head. It was formerly the ford-keeper's cottage and the tenant would have kept watch on people crossing the stream. The ford-keeper was one of Bishop Vesey's 'trusty guides', who succeeded in conducting travellers across the nearby Ebrook on their way between Sutton and Coleshill. The stream in former times was treacherous and Riland Bedford relates in *The Vesey Paper* that: 'Peat, running sand and clay faults are to this day (1893) the cause of stagnation in the flow of the stream, and consequent percolation of the soil. One of the few sound crossing places over the stream of the Ebrook was close to this cottage ...'

From either Peddimore to see his family or Langley to see a friend, William Shakespeare, the famous bard of the 16th century, would have found it no great distance, either afoot or on horseback, to continue on to Sutton Coldfield.

In order for him to reach Sutton, Shakespeare would have descended the hill from Walmley in Wylde Green Road, crossed the ford at the Vesey Cottage, and by way of Old Coles Lane, reached the little town of half-timbered houses clustering around the church on the hill.

Yardley

Yardley today is an ancient parish of Birmingham, but before being incorporated into the city in 1911 it had been a separate manor for almost 1,000 years. It was a large manor some seven miles long and covering an area of over eleven square miles. It belonged to and was administered by Worcestershire, though surrounded by Warwickshire on all sides except to the south-west. Three major highways crossed the manor and because of the great size of the parish it was divided into three parts to ease the administration, using the Warwick and Coventry roads as boundaries.

Blakesley Hall, Yardley

Dense woodland may have deterred early settlers and there is no evidence of any Roman activity in the manor. The earliest reference to Yardley is in AD 972, when it was declared to be a possession of the Benedictine abbey of Pershore in Worcestershire. At this time there are believed to have been some five farms in the manor. Little more is heard of Yardley until the Domesday Book was written and at that time there were probably no more than 60 inhabitants in the manor. During the 12th and 13th centuries the whole area of Arden was subjected to intense clearing and village populations began to increase. Late 13th century documents lead to the assumption that by this date there might well have been in the order of 700 to 800 people living in the parish.

The forest land that was being cleared proved to be slightly more fertile than the sandy soil of the original settlements, but became very heavy and difficult to manage in wet weather. This meant that the farms were largely kept for pasture, particularly as there was a ready market for meat and wool.

Although Pershore Abbey held Yardley it did not provide a

chapel and churchgoers had to travel to the parish of Aston, which would have been a very difficult four mile journey.

The oldest part of the church in Yardley dates from the 13th century, though there may have been an earlier church on a site close by. The church has been extended and modernised through the ages and is still appealing for funds to refurbish and maintain the existing structure. The chancel displays the arms of Pershore Abbey, Tickford, Gatesby and Maxstoke, all of whom were involved in a dispute over the ownership of the church. The dispute dragged on for 100 years until finally in 1347 the church of Yardley was granted to Maxstoke.

In addition to the church a few other buildings survive in the northernmost area of Yardley parish, including a Trust school and Blakesley Hall. The Trust school was probably built in the late 1500s, but of the original building only the west and north side survive. Although the porch is modern, very attractive timbering survives over the top. In Georgian times an extension was built to provide a home for bachelor schoolmasters and the school remained in use until 1908. It is still in use today as a parish community room. Blakesley Hall was originally a moated farmhouse but the present building, which has much impressive timbering, was built by Richard Smallbroke in about 1575. A timber-framed stable block and brick kitchens were added at a later date. The house has now been refurbished in its original style and attracts a large number of visitors and school classes.

The first blacksmith in Yardley was working in about 1275 and there is still a blacksmith in business on a site near the church. Whether this was the original site is not known. Other local crafts to be practised in medieval times were coopering and tanning. The fulling of cloth was believed to have been carried out and in about 1328 there was a weaver of bags in the parish. The river Cole provided enough power for water mills and at one time or another there were believed to have been at least seven, though not all operating at the same time.

Tile making was an important industry in Yardley and it is believed to have been so as early as 1500. It continued to thrive into Stuart times and there were as many as 24 kilns producing tiles and bricks. There was a ready market for tiles and bricks but transport was a problem.

The river Cole was wider and deeper then than it is today and had been an obstacle to access. Parishes were responsible for highway maintenance and they were in a very poor state. One road which was used by local people was a way from the Coventry Road to the church and this had been so difficult to travel along that in the 17th century it was raised to form a causeway. Coventry Road was turnpiked in about 1745 but was still described as bad and dangerous a few years later and was not improved until re-routed in the 1800s. However, just prior to this the Birmingham and Warwick canal was completed and cut through the parish just half a mile south of Coventry Road. This provided cheaper coal for the kilns and an improved route for their goods to Birmingham.

The London to Birmingham railway opened in 1838 and this passed through Stechford, which was in the northern quarter of the parish. A station was built at Stechford some six years later, though it was not until the 1870s that the building of a modern estate near the station began. The Oxford railway with a station in Acocks Green was opened in 1852, so the area began to be a commuter suburb for Birmingham. In the early 1900s electric cars came from the City along the Coventry Road and terminated at the Swan, which is the junction with Church Road. A few years later these were replaced with trams.

Finally, and not without some opposition, the Greater Birmingham Act of 1911 brought Yardley under the authority of the City. In the 1920s and 1930s housing estates began to be built for people who wished to move out of the City and make use of the greatly improved transport systems. In 1926 the Birmingham Corporation provided a bus route to link up its outlaying suburbs and this passed through Yardley and provided transport for the people living in the village to both Stechford and Acocks Green railway stations.

In common with most other parts of the country, house building during the Second World War came to an abrupt halt. The housing boom which followed after the war has resulted in tower blocks, the most recent one being part of a massive redevelopment at the Swan junction. The main Coventry Road is now an expressway and passes underneath the outer circle route linking the suburbs. The tower block now stands on a site formerly occupied by a bakery, and a shopping centre has been built alongside. Opposite is another tower block used as an office centre.

Far less change, however, has taken place in the immediate area of the church, though the road passing by the church was closed to traffic, which was said to be damaging the building. It is now an official conservation area with a recognised society to care for its needs and is today a pleasant area to walk in and to reflect on those who walked the same area a thousand years ago.

Index